Joseph Fitzgerald Molloy

Royalty Restored - or London under Charles II

Vol. II

Joseph Fitzgerald Molloy

Royalty Restored - or London under Charles II
Vol. II

ISBN/EAN: 9783337038823

Printed in Europe, USA, Canada, Australia, Japan

Cover: Foto ©ninafisch / pixelio.de

More available books at **www.hansebooks.com**

CHARLES II. AND HIS QUEEN. [*Frontispiece to Vol. II.*

ROYALTY RESTORED

OR

LONDON UNDER CHARLES II.

BY

J. FITZGERALD MOLLOY

AUTHOR OF
'COURT LIFE BELOW STAIRS; OR, LONDON UNDER THE GEORGES'
'THE LIFE AND ADVENTURES OF PEG WOFFINGTON'
'IT IS NO WONDER,' ETC.

WITH AN ETCHING OF CHARLES II. BY J. GREGO, AND ELEVEN OTHER PORTRAITS

IN TWO VOLUMES
VOL. II.

LONDON
WARD & DOWNEY, PUBLISHERS
12, YORK STREET, COVENT GARDEN
1885
[*All Rights Reserved*]

CONTENTS OF VOL. II.

CHAPTER I.

A cry of fire by night.—Fright and confusion.—The lord mayor is unmanned.—Spread of the flames.—Condition of the streets.—Distressful scenes.—Destruction of the Royal Exchange.—Efforts of the king and the Duke of York.—Strange rumours and alarms. St. Paul's is doomed.—The flames checked.—A ruined city as seen by day and night.—Wretched state of the people.—Investigation into the origin of the fire.—A new city arises 1

CHAPTER II.

The court repairs to Oxford.—Lady Castlemaine's son. Their majesties return to Whitehall. — The king quarrels with his mistress.—Miss Stuart contemplates marriage.—Lady Castlemaine attempts revenge.—Charles makes an unpleasant discovery.—The maid of honour elopes. — His majesty rows down the Thames. — Lady Castlemaine's intrigues. — Fresh quarrels at court.—The king on his knees . . 30

CHAPTER III.

The kingdom in peril.—The chancellor falls under his majesty's displeasure.—The Duke of Buckingham's mimicry.—Lady Castlemaine's malice.—Lord Clarendon's fall.—The Duke of Ormond offends the king's mistress.—She covers him with abuse.—Plots against the Duke of York.—Schemes for a royal divorce.—Moll Davis and Nell Gwynn.—The king and the comedian.—Lady Castlemaine abandons herself to great disorders.—Young Jack Spencer.—The countess intrigues with an acrobat.—Talk of the town.—The mistress created a duchess 50

CHAPTER IV.

Louise de Quérouaille.—The Triple Alliance.—Louise is created Duchess of Portsmouth.—Her grace and the impudent comedian.—Madam Ellen moves in society. The young Duke of St. Albans.—Strange story of the Duchess of Mazarine.—Entertaining the wits at Chelsea.—Luxurious suppers.—Profligacy and wit . 78

CHAPTER V.

A storm threatens the kingdom.—The Duke of York is touched in his conscience.—His interview with Father Simons.—The king declares his mind.—The Duchess of York becomes a catholic.—The circumstances of her death.—The Test Act introduced.—Agitation of the nation.—The Duke of York marries again.—Lord Shaftesbury's schemes.—The Duke of Monmouth.—William of Orange and the Princess Mary.—Their marriage and departure from England 103

CHAPTER VI.

The threatened storm bursts.—History of Titus Oates and Dr. Tonge.—A dark scheme concocted.—The king is warned of danger.—The narrative of a horrid plot laid before the treasurer.—Forged letters.—Titus Oates before the council.—His blunders.—A mysterious murder.—Terror of the citizens.—Lord Shaftesbury's schemes. — Papists are banished from the capital.—Catholic peers committed to the Tower.—Oates is encouraged 132

CHAPTER VII.

Reward for the discovery of murderers. — Bedlow's character and evidence.—His strange story.—Development of the 'horrid plot.'—William Staley is made a victim.—Three Jesuits hung.—Titus Oates pronounced the saviour of his country.—Striving to ruin the queen.—Monstrous story of Bedlow and Oates.—The king protects her majesty.—Five Jesuits executed.—Fresh rumours concerning the papists.—Bill to Exclude the Duke of York.—Lord Stafford is tried.—Scene at Tower Hill.—Fate of the conspirators 165

CHAPTER VIIL

London under Charles II.—Condition and appearance of the thoroughfares.—Coffee is first drunk in the capital.—Taverns and their frequenters.—The city by night.—Wicked people do creep about.—Companies of young gentlemen.—The Duke of Monmouth kills a beadle.—Sir Charles Sedley's frolic.—Stately houses of the nobility.—St. James's Park.—Amusement of the town.—At Bartholomew Fair.—Bull, bear, and dog fights.—Some quaint sports . . 192

CHAPTER IX.

Court customs in the days of the merry monarch.—Dining in public.—The Duke of Tuscany's supper to the king.—Entertainment of guests by mountebanks. Gaming at court.—Lady Castlemaine's losses.—A fatal duel.—Dress of the period.—Riding-habits first seen.—His majesty invents a national costume.—Introduction of the penny post.—Divorce suits are known.—Society of Antiquaries.—Lord Worcester's inventions.—The Duchess of Newcastle . . 224

CHAPTER X.

A period rich in literature.—John Milton's early life.—Writing 'Paradise Lost.'—Its publication and success. His later works and death.—John Dryden gossips with wits and players.—Lord Rochester's revenge.—Elkanah Settle.—John Crowne.—Thomas Otway rich in miseries.—Dryden assailed by villains.—The ingenious Abraham Cowley.—The author of 'Hudibras.'—Young Will Wycherley and Lady Castlemaine. The story of his marriage.—Andrew Marvell, poet and politician.—John Bunyan . . . 257

CHAPTER XI.

Time's flight leaves the king unchanged.—The Rye House conspiracy.—Profligacy of the court.—The three duchesses.—The king is taken ill.—The capital in consternation.—Dr. Ken questions his majesty.—A Benedictine monk is sent for.—Charles professes catholicity and receives the Sacraments.—Farewell to all.—His last night on earth.—Daybreak and death. He rests in peace 297

LIST OF ILLUSTRATIONS.

CHARLES II. AND HIS QUEEN . .	*Frontispiece*	
MARY DAVIS	*to face page*	49
LOUISE DE LA QUÉROUAILLE, DUCHESS OF PORTSMOUTH .	,,	81
NELL GWYNN . . .	,,	102
DUCHESS OF MAZARINE . .	,,	193
DUCHESS OF CLEVELAND . .	,,	273

ROYALTY RESTORED;

OR,

LONDON UNDER CHARLES II.

CHAPTER I.

A cry of fire by night.—Fright and confusion.—The lord mayor is unmanned—Spread of the flames.—Condition of the streets.—Distressful scenes.—Destruction of the Royal Exchange.—Efforts of the king and Duke of York. Strange rumours and alarms.—St. Paul's is doomed.—The flames checked.—A ruined city as seen by day and night.—Wretched state of the people.—Investigation into the origin of the fire.—A new city arises.

SCARCELY had the city of London recovered from the dire effects of the plague, ere a vast fire laid it waste. It happened on the 2nd of September, 1666, that at two o'clock in the morning, the day being Sunday, smoke and flames were seen issuing from the shop of a baker named Faryner, residing in Pudding

Lane, close by Fish Street, in the lower part of the city. The house being built of wood, and coated with pitch, as were likewise those surrounding it, and moreover containing faggots, dried logs, and other combustible materials, the fire spread with great rapidity: so that in a short time not only the baker's premises, but the homesteads which stood next it on either side were in flames.

Accordingly, the watchman's lusty cry of 'Fire, fire, fire!' which had roused the baker and his family in good time to save their lives, was now shouted down the streets with consternation, startling sleepers from their dreams, and awaking them to a sense of peril. Thereon they rose promptly from their beds, and hastily throwing on some clothes, rushed out to rescue their neighbours' property from destruction, and subdue the threatening conflagration.

And speedily was heard the tramp of many feet hurrying to the scene, and the shouting of anxious voices crying for help; and presently the bells of St. Margaret's church close by, ringing with wild uneven peals through the darkness, aroused all far and near to knowledge of the disaster. For already the flames, fanned by a high easterly wind, and fed by the dry timber of the picturesque old dwellings huddled close together, had spread in four directions.

One of these being Thames Street, the consequence was terrible: for the shops and warehouses of this thoroughfare containing inflammable materials, required for the shipping trade, such as oil, pitch, tar, and rosin, the houses at one side the street were immediately wrapped, from basement to garret, in sheets of angry flame. And now flaunting its yellow light skywards, as if exulting in its strength, and triumphing in its mastery over men's efforts, the fire rushed to the church of St. Magnus, a dark solid edifice standing at the foot of London Bridge. The frightened citizens concluded the conflagration must surely end here; or at least that whilst it endeavoured to consume a dense structure such as this, they might succeed in subduing its force; but their hopes were vain. At first the flames shot upwards to the tower of the building, but not gaining hold, retreated as if to obtain fresh strength for new efforts; and presently darting forward again, they seized the woodwork of the belfry windows. A few minutes later the church blazed at every point, and was in itself a colossal conflagration.

From this the fire darted to the bridge, burning the wooden houses built upon it, and the water machines underneath; and likewise creeping up Thames Street, on that side which was yet undemolished. By this time the bells of many churches rang out in sudden fright, as if appealing to heaven for mercy on behalf of the people; and the whole east end of the town rose up in alarm. The entire city seemed threatened with destruction: for the weather having long been dry and warm, prepared the homesteads for their fate; and it was noted some of them, when scorched by the approaching fire, ignited before the flames had time to reach them.

Sir Thomas Bludworth, the lord mayor, now arrived in great haste, but so amazed was he at the sight he beheld, and so bewildered by importunities of those who surrounded him, that he was powerless to act. Indeed, his incapacity to direct, and inability to command, as well as his lack of moral courage, have been heavily and frequently blamed. Being a weak man, fearful of outstepping his authority, he at first forbore pulling down houses standing in the pathway of the flames, as suggested to him; a means that would assuredly have prevented their progress; but when urged to this measure would reply, he 'durst not, without the consent of the owners.' And when at last, after great destruction had taken place, word was brought him from the king to 'spare no house, but pull them down everywhere before the fire,' he cried out 'like a fainting woman,' as Pepys recounts, 'Lord! what can I do? I am spent; people will not obey me.'

Meanwhile, great bodies of the citizens of all classes had been at work; some upon the cumbrous engines, others carrying water, others levelling houses, but all their endeavours seemed powerless to quell the raging flames. And it was notable when first the pipes in the streets were opened, no water could be found, whereon a messenger was sent to the works at Islington, in order to turn on the cocks, so that much time was lost in this manner. All through Sunday morning the flames extended far and wide, and in a few hours three hundred houses were reduced to ashes. Not at midday, nor yet at night, did they give promise of abatement. The strong easterly wind continuing to blow, the conflagration worked its way to Cannon Street: from thence gradually encompassing the dwellings which lay between that thoroughfare and the Thames, till the whole seemed one vast plain of raging fire.

The streets now presented a scene of the uttermost confusion and distress. The affrighted citizens, whose dwellings were momentarily threatened with destruction, hurried to and fro, striving to save those of their families who by reason of infancy, age or illness were unable to help themselves. Women on the eve of childbirth were carried from their beds; mothers with infants clinging to their naked breasts fled from homes which would shelter them no more; the decrepit were borne away on the shoulders of the strong. The narrow thoroughfares were moreover obstructed by furniture dragged from houses, or lowered from windows with a reckless speed that oftentimes destroyed what it sought to preserve. Carts, drays, and horses laden with merchandise jostled each other in their hurried way towards the fields outside the city walls. Men young and vigorous crushed forward with beds or trunks upon their backs; children laboured under the weight of bundles, or rolled barrels of oil, wine, or spirits before them. And the air, rendered suffocating by smoke and flame, was moreover confused by the crackling of consuming timber, the thunder of falling walls, the crushing of glass, the shrieks of women, and the imprecations of men.

And those who lived near the waterside, or in houses on the bridges, hurried their goods and chattels into boats, barges, and lighters, in which they likewise took refuge. For the destruction of wharfs and warehouses, containing stores of most inflammable nature, was brief and desperate. The Thames, now blood-red from reflection of the fierce sky, was covered with craft of all imaginable shape and size. Showers of sparks blown by the high wind fell into the water with hissing sounds, or on the clothes and faces of the people with disastrous and painful effects; and the smoke and heat were hard to bear. And it was remarked that flocks of pigeons, which for generations had found shelter in the eaves and roofs of wooden houses by the riverside, were loath to leave their habitations; and probably fearing to venture afar by reason of the unwonted aspect of the angry sky, lingered on the balconies and abutments of deserted houses, until in some cases, the flames enwrapping them, they fell dead into the waters below.

On Sunday evening Gracechurch Street was on fire; and the flames spread onwards till they reached, and in their fury consumed, the Three Cranes in the Vintry. Night came, but darkness had fled from the city; and for forty miles round all was luminous. And there were many who, in the crimson hue of the heavens, beheld an evidence of God's wrath at the sins of the nation, which it was now acknowledged were many and great.

Throughout Sunday night the fire grew apace, and those who in the morning had carried their belongings to parts of the city which they believed would by distance ensure safety, were now obliged to move them afresh, the devastation extending for miles. Therefore many were compelled to renew their labours, thereby suffering further fatigue; and they now trusted to no protection for their property save that which the open fields afforded. Monday morning came and found the flames yet raging. Not only Gracechurch Street, but Lombard Street, and part of Fenchurch Street, were on fire. Stately mansions, comfortable homes, warehouses of great name, banks of vast wealth, were reduced to charred and blackened walls, or heaps of smoking ruins. Buildings had been pulled down, but now too late to render service; for the insatiable fire, yet fed by a high wind, had everywhere marched over the dried woodwork and mortar as it lay upon the ground, and communicated itself to the next block of buildings; so that its circumvention was regarded as almost an impossibility.

During Monday the flames attacked Cornhill, and then commenced to demolish the Royal Exchange. Having once made an entrance in this stately building, it revelled in triumph; climbing up the walls, roaring along the courts and galleries, and sending through the broken windows volleys of smoke and showers of sparks, which threatened to suffocate and consume those who approached. Then the roof fell with a mighty crash, which seemed for a time to subdue the powerful conflagration; the walls cracked, parted, and fell; statues of kings and queens were flung from their niches; and in a couple of hours this building, which had been the pride and glory of British merchants, was a blackened ruin.

The citizens were now in a state of despair. Upwards of ten thousand houses were in a blaze, the fire extending, according to Evelyn, two miles in length and one in breadth, and the smoke reaching near fifty miles in length. Mansions, churches, hospitals, halls, and schools crumbled into dust as if at blighting touch of some most potent and diabolical magician. Quite hopeless now of quenching the flames, bewildered by loss, and overcome by terror, the citizens, abandoning themselves to despair, made no further effort to conquer this inappeasable fire; but crying aloud in their distraction, behaved as those who had lost their wits. The king and the Duke of York, who on Sunday had viewed the conflagration from the Thames, now alarmed at prospect of the whole capital being laid waste, rode into the city, and by their presence, coolness and example roused the people to fresh exertions. Accordingly, citizens and soldiers worked with renewed energy and courage; whilst his majesty and his brother, the courtiers and the lord mayor, mixed freely with the crowd, commanding and directing them in their labours.

But now a new terror rose up amongst the citizens, for news spread that the Dutch and French—with whom England was then at war—and moreover the papists, whom the people then abhorred, had conspired to destroy the capital. And the suddenness with which the flames had appeared in various places, and the rapidity with which they spread, leading the distracted inhabitants to favour this report, a strong desire for immediate revenge took possession of their hearts.

Accordingly all foreigners were laid hold of, kicked, beaten, and abused by infuriated mobs, from which they were rescued only to be flung into prison. And this conduct was speedily extended to the catholics, even when such were known to be faithful and well-approved good citizens. For though at first it spread as a rumour, it was now received as a certainty that they, in obedience to the wily and most wicked Jesuits, had determined to lay waste an heretical city. Nor were there wanting many ready to bear witness they had seen these dreaded papists fling fire-balls into houses of honest citizens, and depart triumphing in their fiendish deeds. So that when they ventured abroad they were beset by great multitudes, and their lives were imperilled. And news of this distraction, which so forcibly swayed the people, reaching the king, he speedily despatched the members of his privy council to several quarters of the city, that in person they might guard such of his subjects as stood in danger.

Lord Hollis and Lord Ashley were assigned Newgate Market and the streets that lie around, as parts where they were to station themselves. And it happened that riding near the former place they saw a vast number of people gathered together, shouting with great violence, and badly using one who stood in their midst. Whereon they hastened towards the spot and found the ill-treated man to be of foreign aspect. Neither had he hat, cloak, nor sword; his face was covered with blood, his jerkin was torn in pieces, and his person was bedaubed by mud. And on examination it was found he was unable to speak the English tongue; but Lord Hollis, entering into conversation with him in the French language, ascertained he was a servant of the Portuguese ambassador, and knew not of what he was accused, or why he had been maltreated.

Hereon a citizen of good standing pressed forward and alleged he had truly seen this man put his hand in his pocket and throw a fireball into a shop, upon which the house immediately took flame; whereon, being on the other side of the street, he called aloud that the people might stop this abominable villain. Then the citizens had seized upon him, taken away his sword, and used him according to their will. My Lord Hollis explaining this to the foreigner, he was overcome by amazement at the charge; and when asked what he had thrown into the house, made answer he had not flung anything.

But he remembered very well that, walking in the street, he saw a piece of bread upon the ground, which he, as was the custom in his country, took up. Afterwards he laid it upon a shelf in a neighbouring house, which being close by, my Lords Hollis and Ashley, followed by a ense crowd, conducted him thither, and found the bread laid upon a board as he had stated. It was noted the next house but one was on fire, and on inquiry it was ascertained that the worthy citizen, seeing a foreigner place something inside a shop, without tarrying, and immediately after perceiving a dwelling in flames, which in his haste he took to be the same, he had charged the man with commission of this foul deed. But even though many were convinced of his innocence, my Lord Hollis concluded the stranger's life would be in safer keeping if he were committed to prison, which was accordingly done.

Meanwhile the fire continued; and on Monday night and Tuesday it raged with increasing violence. The very heart of the city was now eaten into by this insatiable monster: Soper Lane, Bread Street, Friday Street, Old Change, and Cheapside being in one blaze. It was indeed a spectacle to fill all who beheld it with consternation; but that which followed was yet more terrible, for already St. Paul's Cathedral was doomed to destruction.

Threatened on one side by the flames which devastated Cheapside, and on the other from those creeping steadily up from Blackfriars to this great centre, it was now impossible to save the venerable church, which Evelyn terms 'one of the most ancient pieces of early Christian piety in the world.' Seen by this fierce light, and overhung by a crimson sky, every curve of its dark outline, every stone of its pillars and abutments, every column of its incomparable portico, stood clearly defined, so that never had it looked so stately and magnificent, so vast and majestic, as now, when beheld for the last time.

Too speedily the fire advanced, watched by sorrowful eyes; but even before it had reached the scaffolding which now surrounded the building, the vaulted roof, ignited by showers of sparks, had burst into flames. Then followed a scene unspeakably grand, yet melancholy beyond all telling. In a few moments a pale yellow light had crept along the parapets, sending faint clouds of smoke upwards, as if more forcibly marking the course of destruction. Then came the crackling, hissing sounds of timber yielding to the fire, and soon a great sheet of lead which covered the roof, and was said to measure six acres, melting by degrees, down came on every side a terrible rain of liquid fire that seamed and burned the ground, and carried destruction with it in its swift course towards the Thames.

And now, by reason of the fearful heat, great projections of Portland stone, cornices, and capitals of columns, flew off before the fire had time to reach them. Windows melted in their frames, pillars fell to the ground, ironwork bent as wax; nay, the very pavements around glowed so that neither man nor horse dared tread upon them. And the flames, gradually gaining ground, danced fantastically up and down the scaffolding, and covered the edifice as with one blaze; whilst inside transom beams were snapped asunder, rafters fell with destruction, and the fire roaring through chapels and aisles as in a great furnace, could be heard afar.

And that which had been a Christian shrine was now a smoking ruin.

Raging onward in their fierce career, the flames darted towards such buildings in the neighbourhood as had been previously untouched, so that Paternoster Row, Newgate Street, the Old Bailey and Ludgate Hill were soon in course of destruction. And from the latter spot the conflagration, urged by the wind, rapidly rushed onwards towards Fleet Street. On the other hand, it extended from Cheapside to Ironmongers' Lane, Old Jewry, Lawrence Lane, Milk Street, Wood Street, Gutter Lane, and Foster Lane; and again spreading from Newgate Street, it surrounded and destroyed Christ Church, burned through St. Martin's-le-Grand towards Aldgate, and threatened to continue its triumphant march to the suburbs.

For several miles nothing but raging fire and smoking ruins was visible, for desolation had descended on the city. It was now feared the flames would reach the Palace of Whitehall, and extend towards Westminster Abbey, a consideration which caused much alarm to his majesty, who prized the sacred fane exceedingly. And now the king was determined the orders he had already issued should be obeyed, and that houses standing in direct path of the fire should be demolished by gunpowder; so that, a greater gap being effected than any previously made by pulling them down, the conflagration might have no further material wherewith to strengthen and feed its further progress.

This plan, Evelyn states, had been proposed by some stout seamen early enough to have saved nearly the whole city; 'but this some tenacious and avaricious men, aldermen, etc., would not permit, because their houses would have been the first.' Now, however, this remedy was tried, and with greater despatch, because the fire threatened the Tower and the powder magazine it contained. And if the flames once reached this, London Bridge would assuredly be destroyed, the vessels in the river torn and sunk, and incalculable damage to life and property effected.

Accordingly Tower Street, which had already become ignited, was, under supervision of the king, blown up in part, and the fire happily brought to an end by this means in that part of the town. And, moreover, on Wednesday morning the east wind, which had continued high from Sunday night, now subsided, so that the flames lost much of their vehemence, and by means of explosions were more easily mastered at Leadenhall and in Holborn, and likewise at the Temple, to which places they had spread during Wednesday and Thursday.

During these latter days, the king and the Duke of York betrayed great vigilance, and laboured with vast activity; the latter especially, riding from post to post, by his example inciting those whose courage had deserted them, and by his determination overcoming destruction. On Thursday the dread conflagration, after raging for five consecutive days and nights, was at length conquered.

On Friday morning the sun rose like a ball of crimson fire above a scene of blackness, ruin, and desolation. Whole streets were levelled to the ground, piles of charred stones marked where stately churches had stood, smoke rose in clouds from smouldering embers. With sorrowful hearts many citizens traversed the scene of desolation that day; amongst others Pepys and Evelyn.

The latter recounts that 'the ground and air, smoake and fiery vapour, continu'd so intense, that my haire was almost sing'd, and my feete unsuffurably surbated. The people who now walk'd about ye ruines appear'd like men in some dismal desert, or rather in some greate citty laid waste by a cruel enemy; to which was added that stench that came from some poore creatures' bodies, beds, and other combustible goods.'

It would have been impossible to have traced the original course of the streets, but that some gable, pinnacle, or portion of walls, of churches, halls, or mansions, indicated where they had stood. The narrower thoroughfares were completely blocked by rubbish; massive iron chains, then used to prevent traffic at night in the streets, were melted, as were likewise iron gates of prisons, and the hinges of strong doors. Goods stored away in cellars and subterranean passages of warehouses yet smouldered, emitting foul odours; wells were completely choked, fountains were dried at their sources. The statues of monarchs, which had adorned the Exchange, were smashed; that of its founder, Sir Thomas Gresham, alone remaining entire. The ruins of St. Paul's, with its walls standing black and cheerless, presented in itself a most melancholy spectacle. Its pillars were embedded in ashes, its cornices irretrievably destroyed, its great bell reduced to a shapeless mass of metal; whilst its general air of desolation was heightened by the fact that a few monuments, which had escaped destruction, rose abruptly from amidst the charred *débris*.

But if the ruins of the capital looked sad by day, their appearance was far more appalling when seen by light of the moon, which rose nightly during the week following this great calamity. From the city gates, standing gaunt, black, and now unguarded, to the Temple, the level waste seemed sombre as a funeral pall; whilst the Thames, stripped of wharves and warehouses, quaintly gabled homes, and comfortable inns—wont to cast pleasant lights and shadows on its surface—now swept past the blackened ruins a melancholy river of white waters.

In St. George's Fields, Moorfields, and far as Highgate for several miles, citizens of all degrees, to the number of two hundred thousand, had gathered: sleeping in the open fields, or under canvas tents, or in wooden sheds which they hurriedly erected. Some there were amongst them who had been used to comfort and luxury, but who were now without bed or board, or aught to cover them save the clothes in which they had hastily dressed when fleeing from the fire. And to many it seemed as if they had only been saved from one calamity to die by another: for they had nought wherewith to satisfy their hunger, yet had too much pride to seek relief.

And whilst yet wildly distracted by their miserable situation, weary from exhaustion, and nervous from lack of repose, a panic arose in their midst which added much to their distress. For suddenly news was spread that the French, Dutch and English papists were marching on them, prepared to cut their throats. At which, broken-spirited as they were, they rose up, and leaving such goods as they had saved, rushed towards Westminster to seek protection from their imaginary foes. On this, the king sought to prove the falsity of their alarm, and with infinite difficulty persuaded them to return to the fields: whence he despatched troops of soldiers, whose presence helped to calm their fears.

And the king having, moreover, tender compassion for their wants, speedily sought to supply them. He therefore summoned a council that it might devise means of relief; and as a result, it published a proclamation ordering that bread and all other provisions, such as could be furnished, should be daily and constantly brought, not only to the markets formerly in use, but also to Clerkenwell, Islington, Finsbury Fields, Mile End Green, and Ratcliffe, for greater convenience of the citizens. For those who were unable to buy provisions, the king commanded the victualler of his navy to send bread into Moorfields, and distribute it amongst them. And as divers distressed people had saved some of their goods, of which they knew not where to dispose, he ordered that churches, chapels, schools, and such like places in and around Westminster, should be free and open to receive and protect them. He likewise directed that all cities and towns should, without contradiction or opposition, receive the citizens and permit them free exercise of their manual labours: he promising, when the present exigency had passed away, to take care the said persons should be no burden to such towns as received them.

The people were therefore speedily relieved. Many of them found refuge with their friends and relatives in the country, and others sought homes in the districts of Westminster and Southwark: so that in four days from the termination of the fire, there was scarce a person remaining in the fields, where such numbers had taken refuge.

The first hardships consequent to the calamity having passed away, people were anxious to trace the cause of their sufferings, which they were unwilling to consider accidental. A rumour therefore sprang up, that the great fire resulted from a wicked plot, hatched by Jesuits, for the destruction of an heretical city. At this the king was sorely troubled; for though there was no evidence which led him to place faith in the report, yet a great body of the citizens and many members of his council held true. Therefore, in order to appease such doubts as arose in his mind, and likewise to satisfy the people, he appointed his privy council to sit morning and evening to inquire into the matter, and examine evidences set forth against those who had been charged with the outrage and cast into prison during the conflagration.

And in order that the investigation might be conducted with greater rigour, he sent into the country for the lord chief justice, who was dreaded by all for his unflinching severity. The lord chancellor, in his account of these transactions, assures us many of the witnesses who gave evidence against those indicted with firing the capital 'were produced as if their testimony would remove all doubts, but made such senseless relations of what they had been told, without knowing the condition of the persons who told them, or where to find them, that it was a hard matter to forbear smiling at their declarations.' Amongst those examined was one Roger Hubert, who accused himself of having deliberately set the city on fire. This man, then in his twenty-fifth year, was son of a watchmaker residing in Rouen. Hubert had practised the same trade both in that town and in London, and was believed by his fellow workmen to be demented. When brought before the chief justice and privy council, Hubert with great coolness stated he had set the first house on fire: for which act he had been paid a year previously in Paris. When asked who had hired him to accomplish this evil deed, he replied he did not know, for he had never seen the man before: and when further questioned regarding the sum he had received, he declared it was but one pistole, but he had been promised five pistoles more when he should have done his work. These ridiculous answers, together with some contradictory statements he made, inclined many persons, amongst whom was the chief justice, to doubt his confession. Later on in his examinations, he was asked if he knew where the house had stood which he set on fire, to which he replied in the affirmative, and on being taken into the city, pointed out the spot correctly.

In the eyes of many this was regarded as proof of his guilt; though others stated that, having lived in the city, he must necessarily become acquainted with the position of the baker's shop. Opinion was therefore somewhat divided regarding him. The chief justice told the king 'that all his discourse was so disjointed that he did not believe him guilty.' Yet, having voluntarily accused himself of a monstrous deed, and being determined as it seemed to rid himself of life, he was condemned to death and speedily executed.

Lord Clarendon says: 'Neither the judges nor any present at the trial did believe him guilty; but that he was a poor distracted wretch, weary of his life, and chose to part with it in this way. Certain it is that upon the strictest examination that could be afterwards made by the king's command, and then by the diligence of the House, that upon the jealousy and rumour made a committee, that was very diligent and solicitous to make that discovery, there was never any probable evidence (that poor creature's only excepted) that there was any other cause of that woeful fire than the displeasure of God Almighty: the first accident of the beginning in a baker's house, where there was so great a stock of faggots, and the neighbourhood of such combustible matter, of pitch and rosin, and the like, led it in an instant from house to house, through Thames Street, with the agitation of so terrible a wind to scatter and disperse it.'

But belief that the dreaded papists had set fire to the city, lingered in the minds of many citizens. When the city was rebuilt, this opinion found expression in an inscription cut over the doorway of a house opposite the spot where the fire began, which ran as follows:

'Here, by the permission of heaven, hell broke loose on this protestant city from the malicious hearts of barbarous papists, by the hand of their agent Hubert, who confessed, and on the ruins of this place declared the fact, for which he was hanged. Erected in the mayoralty of Sir Patience Ward, Knight.'

The loss caused by this dreadful conflagration was estimated at ten million sterling. According to a certificate of Jonas Moore and Ralph Gatrix, surveyors appointed to examine the ruins, the fire overrun 373 acres within the walls, burning 13,200 houses, 89 parish churches, numerous chapels, the Royal Exchange, Custom House, Guildhall, Blackwell Hall, St. Paul's Cathedral, Bridewell, fifty-two halls of the city companies, and three city gates.

As speedily as might be, the king and his

parliament, then sitting at Oxford, sought to restore the city on a scale vastly superior to its former condition. And the better to effect this object, an act of parliament was passed that public buildings should be rebuilt with public money, raised by a tax on coals; that the churches and the cathedral of St. Paul's should be reconstructed from their foundations; that bridges, gates and prisons should be built anew; the streets made straight and regular, such as were steep made level, such as were narrow made wide; and, moreover, that every house should be built with party walls, such being of stone or brick, and all houses raised to equal height in front.

And these rules being observed, a stately and magnificent city rose phœnix-like from ruins of the old; so that there was naught to remind the inhabitants of their great calamity save the monument. This, designed by Sir Christopher Wren, and built at a cost of fourteen thousand five hundred pounds, was erected near where the fire broke out, the better to perpetuate a memory of this catastrophe in the minds of future generations, which purpose it fulfils unto this day.

CHAPTER II.

The court repairs to Oxford.—Lady Castlemaine's son.—Their majesties return to Whitehall.—The king quarrels with his mistress.—Miss Stuart contemplates marriage.—Lady Castlemaine attempts revenge.—Charles makes an unpleasant discovery.—The maid of honour elopes.—His majesty rows down the Thames.—Lady Castlemaine's intrigues.—Fresh quarrels at court.—The king on his knees.

THE while such calamities befell the citizens, the king continued to divert himself in his usual fashion. On the 29th of June, 1665, whilst death strode apace through the capital, reaping full harvests as he went, their majesties left Whitehall for Hampton Court. From here they repaired to Salisbury, and subsequently to Oxford, where Charles took up his residence in Christchurch, and the queen at Merton College.

Removed from harrowing scenes of ghastliness

and distress, the court made merry. Joined by fair women and gallant men, their majesties played at bowls and tennis in the grassy meads of the college grounds; rode abroad in great hawking parties; sailed through summer days upon the smooth waters of the river Isis; and by night held revelry in the massive-beamed oak-panelled halls, from which scarce five-score candles served to chase all gloom.

It happened whilst life thus happily passed, at pleasant full-tide flow, my Lady Castlemaine, who resided in the same college with her majesty, gave birth on the 28th of December to another son, duly baptized George Fitzroy, and subsequently created Duke of Northumberland. By this time, the plague having subsided in the capital, and all danger of infection passed away, his majesty was anxious to reach London, yet loath to leave his mistress, whom he visited every morning, and to whom he exhibited the uttermost tenderness. And his tardiness to return becoming displeasing to the citizens, and they being aware of its cause, it was whispered in taverns and cried in the streets, 'The king cannot go away till my Lady

Castlemaine be ready to come along with him;' which truth was found offensive on reaching the royal ears.

Towards the end of January, 1666, he returned to Whitehall; and a month later the queen, who had been detained by a miscarriage, joined him. And once more the thread of life was taken up by the court at the point where it had been broken, and woven into the motley web of its strange history. Unwearied by time, unsatiated by familiarity, the king yet continued his intrigue with the imperious Castlemaine, and with great longing he likewise made love to the beautiful Stuart. But yet his pursuit of pleasure was not always attended by happiness; inasmuch as he found himself continually involved in quarrels with the countess, which in turn covered him with ridicule in the eyes of his courtiers, and earned him contempt in the opinions of his subjects.

One of these disturbances, which occurred soon after his return from Oxford, commenced at a royal drawing-room, in presence of the poor slighted queen and ladies of the court. It happened in the course of conversation her majesty remarked to the countess she feared the king had taken cold by staying so late at her lodgings; to which speech my Lady Castlemaine with some show of temper answered aloud before all, 'he did not stay so late abroad with her, for he went betimes thence, though he do not before one, two, or three in the morning, but must stay somewhere else.' The king, who had entered the apartment whilst she was speaking, came up to her, and displeased with the insinuations she expressed, declared she was a bold, impertinent woman, and moreover bade her begone from the court, and not return until he sent for her. Accordingly she whisked from the drawing-room, and drove at once to Pall Mall, where she hired apartments.

Her indignation at being addressed by Charles in such a manner before the whole court, was sufficiently great to beget strong desires for revenge; when she swore she would be even with him and print his letters to her for public sport. In cooler moments, however, she abandoned this idea; and in course of two or three days, not hearing from his majesty, she despatched a message to him, not entreating pardon, but asking permission to send for her furniture and belongings. To this the monarch, who had begun to miss her presence and long for her return, replied she must first come and view them; and then, impatient for reconciliation, he sought her, and they became friends once more. And by way of sealing the bond of pacification, the king soon after agreed to pay her debts, amounting to the sum of thirty thousand pounds, which had been largely incurred by presents bestowed by her upon her lovers.

His majesty was not only rendered miserable by the constant caprices and violent temper of the countess, but likewise by the virtue and coldness Miss Stuart betrayed since her return from Oxford. The monarch was sorely troubled to account for her bearing, and attributing it to jealousy, sought to soothe her supposed uneasiness by increasing his chivalrous attentions. Her change of behaviour, however, proceeded from another cause. The fair Stuart, though childlike in manner, was shrewd at heart; and was moreover guided invariably by her mother, a lady who reaped wisdom from familiarity with courts. Therefore the maid of honour, seeing she had given the world occasion to think she had lost her virtue, declared she was ready to 'marry any gentleman of fifteen hundred a year that would have her in honour.'

This determination she was obliged to keep secret from the king, lest his anger should fall upon such as sought her, and so interfere with her matrimonial prospects. Now with such intentions in her mind she pondered well on an event which had happened to her, such as no woman who has had like experience ever forgets; namely, that amongst the many who professed to love her, one had proposed to marry her. This was Charles Stuart, fourth Duke of Richmond, a man possessed of neither physical gifts nor mental abilities; who was, moreover, a widower, and a sot.

However, the position which her union with him would ensure was all she could desire; and he renewing his suit at this time, she consequently consented to marry him. Now, though it was probable she could keep her design from knowledge of her royal lover, it was scarcely possible she could hide it from observation of his mistress. And the latter, knowing the extent to which fair Frances Stuart shared his majesty's heart, and being likewise aware of the coldness with which his protestations were by her received, scorned the king and detested the maid. Lady Castlemaine therefore resolved to use her knowledge of Miss Stuart's contemplated marriage, for purpose of enraging the jealousy of the one, and destroying the influence of the other. In order to accomplish such desirable ends she quietly awaited her opportunity. This came in due time.

It happened one evening when his majesty had been visiting Frances Stuart in her apartments, and had returned to his own in a condition of ill-humour and disappointment, the countess, who had been some days out of favour, suddenly presented herself before him, and in a bantering tone, accompanied by ironical smiles, addressed him.

'I hope,' said she, 'I may be allowed to pay you my homage, although the angelic Stuart has forbidden you to see me at my own house. I will not make use of reproaches and expostulations which would disgrace myself; still less will I endeavour to excuse frailties which nothing can justify, since your constancy for me deprives me of all defence, considering I am the only person you have honoured with your tenderness, who has made herself unworthy of it by ill-conduct. I come now, therefore, with no other intent than to comfort and condole with you upon the affliction and grief into which the coldness or new-fashioned chastity of the inhuman Stuart has reduced your majesty.'

Having delivered herself of this speech she laughed loud and heartily, as if vastly amused at the tenour of her words; and then before the impatient monarch had time to reply, continued in the same tone, with quickening breath and flashing eyes, 'Be not offended that I take the liberty of laughing at the gross manner in which you are imposed upon; I cannot bear to see that such particular affection should make you the jest of your own court, and that you should be ridiculed with such impunity. I know that the affected Stuart has sent you away under pretence of some indisposition, or perhaps some scruple of conscience; and I come to acquaint you that the Duke of Richmond will soon be with her, if he is not there already. I do not desire you to believe what I say, since it might be suggested either through resentment or envy. Only follow me to her apartment, either that, no longer trusting calumny and malice, you may honour her with a just preference, if I accuse her falsely; or, if my information be true, you may no longer be the dupe of a pretended prude, who makes you act so unbecoming and ridiculous a part.'

The king, overwhelmed with astonishment, was irresolute in action; but Lady Castlemaine, determined on not being deprived of her anticipated triumph, took him by the hand and forcibly pulled him towards Miss Stuart's apartments. The maid of honour's servants, surprised at his majesty's return, were unable to warn their mistress without his knowledge; whilst one of them, in pay of the countess, found means of secretly intimating to her that the Duke of Richmond was already in Miss Stuart's chamber. Lady Castlemaine, having with an air of exultation led the king down the gallery from his apartments to the threshold of Miss Stuart's door, made him a low courtesy savouring more of irony than homage, bade him good-night, and with a subtle smile promptly retired.

The scene which followed is best painted by Hamilton's pen. 'It was near midnight; the king on his way met the chambermaids, who respectfully opposed his entrance, and, in a very low voice, whispered his majesty that Miss Stuart had been very ill since he left her; but that being gone to bed, she was, God be thanked, in a very fine sleep. "That I must see," said the king, pushing her back, who had posted herself in his way. He found Miss Stuart in bed, indeed, but far from being asleep; the Duke of Richmond was seated at her pillow, and in all probability was less inclined to sleep than herself. The perplexity of the one party, and the rage of the other, were such as may easily be imagined upon such a surprise. The king, who of all men was one of the most mild and gentle, testified his resentment to the Duke of Richmond in such terms as he had never before used. The duke was speechless and almost petrified; he saw his master and his king justly irritated. The first transports which rage inspires on such occasions are dangerous. Miss Stuart's window was very convenient for a sudden revenge, the Thames flowing close beneath it; he cast his eyes upon it, and seeing those of the king more incensed and fired with indignation than he thought his nature capable of, he made a profound bow, and retired without replying a single word to the vast torrent of threats and menaces that were poured upon him.

'Miss Stuart having a little recovered from her first surprise, instead of justifying herself, began to talk in the most extravagant manner, and said everything that was most capable to inflame the king's passion and resentment: that if she were not allowed to receive visits from a man of the Duke of Richmond's rank, who came with honourable intentions, she was a slave in a free country; that she knew of no engagement that could prevent her from disposing of her hand as she thought proper; but, however, if this were not permitted her in his dominions, she did not believe that there was any power on earth that could hinder her from going over to France, and throwing herself into a convent, to enjoy there that tranquillity which was denied her in his court. The king, sometimes furious with anger, sometimes relenting at her tears, and sometimes terrified at her menaces, was so greatly agitated that he knew not how to answer either the nicety of a creature who wanted to act the part of Lucretia under his own eye, or the assurance with which she had the effrontery to reproach him. In this suspense love had almost entirely vanquished all his resentments, and had nearly induced him to throw himself upon his knees, and entreat pardon for the injury he had done her, when she desired him to retire, and leave her in repose, at least for the remainder of that night, without offending those who had either accompanied him, or conducted him to her apartments, by a longer visit. This impertinent request provoked and irritated him to the highest degree: he went out abruptly, vowing never to see her more, and passed the most restless and uneasy night he had ever experienced since his restoration.'

Next morning, his majesty sent orders to the Duke of Richmond to quit the court, and never appear again in his presence. His grace, however, stayed not to receive this message, having betaken himself with all possible speed into the country. Miss Stuart, who likewise feared the king's resentment, hastened to the queen, and throwing herself at her majesty's feet, entreated forgiveness for the pain and uneasiness she had caused her in the past, and besought her care and protection in the future.

She then laid bare her intentions of marrying the Duke of Richmond, who had loved her long, and was anxious to wed her soon; but since the discovery of his addresses had caused his banishment, and created disturbances prejudicial to her good name, she begged the queen would obtain his majesty's consent to her retiring from the vexations of a court to the tranquillity of a convent. The queen raised her up, mingled her tears with those of the troubled maid, and promised to use her endeavours towards averting the king's displeasure.

On consideration, however, the fair Stuart did not wait to hear his majesty's reproaches, or receive his entreaties; for the duke, being impatient to gain his promised bride, quietly returned to town, and secretly communicated with her. It was therefore agreed between them she should steal away from the palace, meet him at the 'Bear at the Bridge Foot,' situated on the Southwark side of the river, where he would have a coach awaiting her, in order they might ride away to his residence at Cobham Hall, near Gravesend, and then be legally and happily united in the holy bonds of matrimony. And all fell out as had been arranged: the time being the month of March, 1667.

Now when the king discovered her flight, his anger knew no bounds, though it sought relief in uttering many violent threats against the duke, and in sending word to the duchess he would see her no more. In answer to this message, she, with some show of spirit, returned him the jewels he had given her, principal amongst which were a necklace of pearls, valued at over a thousand pounds, and a pair of diamond pendants of rare lustre.

Neither she nor her husband paid much heed to the royal menaces, for before a year elapsed they both returned to town, and took up their residence at Somerset House. Here, as

Pepys records, she kept a great court, 'she being visited for her beauty's sake by people, as the queen is at nights: and they say also she is likely to go to court again, and there put my Lady Castlemaine's nose out of joint. God knows that would make a great turn.' But to such proposals as were made regarding her return to Whitehall, her husband would not pay heed, and she therefore remained a stranger to its drawing-rooms for some time longer. And when two years later she appeared there, her beauty had lost much of its famed lustre, for meantime she was overtaken by smallpox, a scourge ever prevalent in the capital. During her illness the king paid her several visits, and was sorely grieved that the loveliness he so much prized should be marred by foul disease. But on her recovery, the disfigurement she suffered scarce lessened his admiration, and by no means abated his love; which seemed to have gained fresh force from the fact of its being interrupted awhile.

This soon became perceptible to all, and rumour whispered that the young duchess would shortly return to Whitehall in a position which she had declined before marriage. And amongst other stories concerning the king's love for her, it was common talk that one fair evening in May, when he had ordered his coach to be ready that he might take an airing in the park, he, on a sudden impulse, ran down the broad steps leading from his palace gardens to the riverside. Here, entering a boat alone, he rowed himself adown the placid river now crossed by early shadows, until he came to Somerset House, where his lady-love dwelt; and finding the garden-door locked, he, in his impatience to be with her, clambered over the wall and sought her. Two months after the occurrence of this incident, the young duchess was appointed a lady of the bedchamber to the queen, and therefore had apartments at Whitehall. There was little doubt now entertained she any longer rejected his majesty's love; and in order to remove all uncertainties on the point which might arise in her husband's mind, the king one night, when he had taken over much wine, boasted to the duke of her complaisancy. Lord Dartmouth, who tells this story, says this happened 'at Lord Townshend's, in Norfolk, as my uncle told me, who was present.' Soon after his grace accepted an honourable exile as ambassador to Denmark, in which country he died.

During the absence of the Duchess of Richmond, my Lady Castlemaine, then in the uninterrupted possession of power, led his majesty a sorry life. Her influence, indeed, seemed to increase with time, until her victim became a laughing stock to the heartless, and an object of pity to the wise. Mr. Povy, whose office as a member of the Tangier Commission brought him into continual contact with the court, and whose love of gossip made him observant of all that passed around him, in telling of 'the horrid effeminacy of the king,' said that 'upon any falling out between my Lady Castlemaine's nurse and her woman, my lady hath often said she would make the king make them friends, and they would be friends and be quiet—which the king had been fain to do.' Nor did such condescension on his majesty's part incline his mistress to treat him with more respect; for in the quarrels which now became frequent betwixt them she was wont to term him a fool, in reply to the kingly assertion that she was a jade.

The disturbances which troubled the court were principally caused by her infidelities to him, and his subsequent jealousies of her. Chief among those who shared her intrigues at this time was Harry Jermyn, with whom she renewed her intimacy from time to time, without the knowledge of his majesty. The risks she frequently encountered in pursuit of her amours abounded in comedy. Speaking of Harry Jermyn, Pepys tells us the king 'had like to have taken him abed with her, but that he was fain to creep under the bed into the closet.' It being now rumoured that Jermyn was about to wed my Lady Falmouth, the countess's love for one whom she might for ever lose received a fresh impulse, which made her reckless of concealment. The knowledge of her passion, therefore, coming to Charles's ears, a bitter feud sprang up between them, during which violent threats and abusive language were freely exchanged.

At this time my lady was far gone with child, a fact that soon came bubbling up to the angry surface of their discourse; for the king avowed he would not own it as his offspring. On hearing this, her passion became violent beyond all decent bounds. 'God damn me, but you shall own it!' said she, her cheeks all crimson and her eyes afire; and moreover she added, 'she should have it christened in the Chapel Royal, and owned as his, or otherwise she would bring it to the gallery in Whitehall, and dash its brains out before his face.'

After she had hectored him almost out of his wits, this beautiful fury fled in a state of wild excitement from the palace, and took up her abode at the residence of Sir Daniel Harvey, the ranger of Richmond Park. News of this scene spread rapidly through the court, and was subsequently discussed in the coffee-houses and taverns all over the town, where great freedom was made with the lady's name, and great sport of the king's passion. And now it was said the monarch had parted with his mistress for ever, concerning which there was much rejoicement and some doubt. For notwithstanding the king had passed his word to this effect, yet it was known though his spirit was willing his flesh was weak. Indeed, three days had scarcely passed when, mindful of her temper, he began to think his words had been harsh, and,

MARY DAVIS.
(From the Picture by Sir Peter Lely).

conscious of her power, he concluded his vows had been rash. He therefore sought her once more, but found she was not inclined to relent, until, as Pepys was assured, this monarch of most feeble spirit, this lover of most ardent temper, 'sought her forgiveness upon his knees, and promised to offend her no more.'

CHAPTER III.

The kingdom in peril.—The chancellor falls under his majesty's displeasure. — The Duke of Buckingham's mimicry.—Lady Castlemaine's malice.—Lord Clarendon's fall.—The Duke of Ormond offends the royal favourite.—She covers him with abuse.—Plots against the Duke of York.—Schemes for a royal divorce.—Moll Davis and Nell Gwynn.—The king and the comedian.—Lady Castlemaine abandons herself to great disorders.—Young Jack Spencer.—The countess intrigues with an acrobat.—Talk of the town.—The mistress created a duchess.

AT this time the kingdom stood in uttermost danger, being brought to that condition by his majesty's negligence towards its concerns. The peril was, moreover, heightened from the fact of the king being impatient to rid himself of those who had the nation's credit at heart, and sought to uphold its interests. To this end he was led in part by his own inclinations, and furthermore by his friends' solicitations. Foremost amongst those with whose services he was anxious to dispense, were the chancellor, my Lord Clarendon, and the lord lieutenant of Ireland, his grace the Duke of Ormond.

The king's displeasure against these men, who had served his father loyally, himself faithfully, and their country honestly, was instigated through hatred borne them by my Lady Castlemaine. From the first both had bewailed the monarch's connection with her, and the evil influence she exercised over him. Accordingly, after the pattern of honest men, they had set their faces against her.

Not only, as has already been stated, would the chancellor refuse to let any document bearing her name pass the great seal, but he had often prevailed with the king to alter resolutions she had persuaded him to form. And moreover had his lordship sinned in her eyes by forbidding his wife to visit or hold intercourse with her. These were sufficient reasons to arouse the hatred and procure the revenge of this malicious woman, who was now virtually at the head of the kingdom. For awhile, however, Charles, mindful of the services the chancellor had rendered him, was unwilling to thrust him from his high place. But as time sped, and the machinations of a clique of courtiers in league with the countess were added to her influence, the chancellor's power wavered. And finally, when he was suspected of stepping between his majesty and his unlawful pleasures—concerning which more shall be said anon—he fell.

At the head and front of the body which plotted against Lord Clarendon, pandered to Lady Castlemaine, and, for its own purposes— politically and socially—sought to control the king, was his grace the Duke of Buckingham. This witty courtier and his friends, when assembled round the pleasant supper table spread in the countess's apartments, and honoured almost nightly by the presence of the king, delighted to vent the force of their humour upon the chancellor, and criticize his influence over the monarch until Charles smarted from their words. In the height of their mirth, if his majesty declared he would go a journey, walk in a certain direction, or perform some trivial action next day, those around him would lay a wager he would not fulfil his intentions; and when asked why they had arrived at such conclusions, they would reply, because the chancellor would not permit him. On this, another would remark with mock gravity, he thought there were no grounds for such an imputation, though, indeed, he could not deny it was universally believed abroad his majesty was implicitly governed by Lord Clarendon. The king, being keenly sensitive to remarks doubting his authority, and most desirous of appearing his own master, would exclaim on such occasions that the chancellor 'had served him long, and understood his business, in which he trusted him; but in any other matter than his business, he had no more credit with him than any other man.' And presently the Duke of Buckingham—who possessed talents of mimicry to a surpassing degree—would arise, and, screwing his face into ridiculous contortions, and shaking his wig in a manner that burlesqued wisdom to perfection, deliver some ludicrous speech brimming with mirth and indecencies, assuming the grave air and stately manner of the chancellor the while. And finally, to make the caricature perfect, Tom Killigrew, hanging a pair of bellows before him by way of purse, and preceded by a friend carrying a fireshovel to represent a mace, would walk round the room with the slow determined tread peculiar to Lord Clarendon. At these performances the king, his mistress, and his courtiers would laugh loud and long in chorus, with which was mingled sounds of chinking glasses and flowing wine.*

In this manner was the old man's power undermined; but a circumstance which hastened his fall occurred in the early part of 1667. In that year Lady Castlemaine had, for a valuable consideration, disposed of a place at court, which ensured the purchaser a goodly salary. However, before the bargain could finally be ratified, it was necessary the appointment should pass the great seal. This the chancellor would not permit, and accompanied his refusal by remarking, 'he thought this woman would sell everything shortly.' His speech being repeated to her, she, in great rage, sent him word she 'had disposed of this place, and had no doubt in a

* 'Came my lord chancellor (the Earl of Clarendon) and his lady, his purse and mace borne before him, to visit me.'
—Evelyn's 'Diary.'

little time to dispose of his.' And so great was the malice she bore him, that she railed against him openly and in all places; nor did she scruple to declare in the queen's chamber, in the presence of much company, 'that she hoped to see his head upon a stake, to keep company with those of the regicides on Westminster Hall.'

And some political movements now arising, the history of which lies not within the province of this work, the king seized upon them as an excuse for parting with his chancellor. The monarch complained that my Lord Clarendon 'was so imperious that he would endure no contradiction; that he had a faction in the House of Commons that opposed everything that concerned his majesty's service, if it were not recommended to them by him; and that he had given him very ill advice concerning the parliament, which offended him most.'

Therefore there were rumours in the air that the chancellor's fall was imminent; nor were the efforts of his son-in-law, the Duke of York, able to protect him, for the friends of my Lady Castlemaine openly told his majesty 'it would not consist with his majesty's honour to be hectored out of his determination to dismiss the chancellor by his brother, who was wrought upon by his wife's crying.' It therefore happened on the 26th of August, 1667, as early as ten o'clock in the morning, Lord Clarendon waited at Whitehall on the king, who presently, accompanied by his brother, received him with characteristic graciousness. Whereon the old man, acknowledging the monarch's courtesy, said he 'had no suit to make to him, nor the least thought to dispute with him, or to divert him from the resolution he had taken; but only to receive his determination from himself, and most humbly to beseech him to let him know what fault he had committed, that had drawn this severity upon him from his majesty.'

In answer to this Charles said he must always acknowledge 'he had served him honestly and faithfully, and that he did believe never king had a better servant; that he had taken this resolution for his good and preservation, as well as for his own convenience and security; that he was sorry the business had taken so much air, and was so publicly spoken of, that he knew not how to change his purpose.' To these words of fair seeming the troubled chancellor replied by doubting if the sudden dismissal of an old servant who had served the crown full thirty years, without any suggestion of crime, but rather with a declaration of innocence, would not call his majesty's justice and good nature into question. He added that men would not know how to serve him, when they should see it was in the power of three or four persons who had never done him any notable service to dispose him to ungracious acts. And finally, he made bold to cast some reflections upon my Lady Castlemaine, and give his majesty certain warnings regarding her influence.

At this the king, not being well pleased, rose up, and the interview, which had lasted two hours, terminated. Lord Clarendon tells us so much concerning his memorable visit, to which Pepys adds a vivid vignette picture of his departure. When my lord passed from his majesty's presence into the privy garden, my Lady Castlemaine, who up to that time had been in bed, 'ran out in her smock into her aviary looking into Whitehall—and thither her woman brought her nightgown—and stood joying herself at the old man's going away; and several of the gallants of Whitehall, of which there were many staying to see the chancellor return, did talk to her in her birdcage—among others Blaneford, telling her she was the bird of paradise.'

A few days after this occurrence the king sent Secretary Morrice to the chancellor's house, with a warrant under a sign manual to require and receive the great seal. This Lord Clarendon at once delivered him with many expressions of duty which he bade the messenger likewise convey his majesty. And no sooner had Morrice handed the seals to the king than Baptist May, keeper of the privy purse, and friend of my Lady Castlemaine, sought the monarch, and falling upon his knees, kissed his hand and congratulated him on his riddance of the chancellor. 'For now,' said he, availing himself of the liberty Charles permitted his friends, 'you will be king—what you have never been before.' Finally, the chancellor was, through influence of his enemies, impeached in the House of Commons; and to such length did they pursue him, that he was banished the kingdom by act of parliament.

His grace the Duke of Ormond was the next minister whom my Lady Castlemaine, in the strength of her evil influence, sought to undermine. By reason of an integrity rendering him too loyal to the king to pander to his majesty's mistress, he incurred her displeasure in many ways; but especially by refusing to gratify her cupidity. It happened she had obtained from his majesty a warrant granting her the Phœnix Park, Dublin, and the mansion situated therein, which had always been placed at service of the lords lieutenants, and was the only summer residence at their disposal. The duke, therefore, boldly refusing to pass the warrant, stopped the grant.* This so enraged the countess, that soon after, when his grace returned to England, she, on meeting him in one of the apartments in Whitehall, greeted him with a torrent of abusive language and bitter reproaches, such as the rancour of her heart could suggest, or the license of her tongue utter, and

* According to O'Connor's 'Bibliotheca Stowensis,' Lady Castlemaine soon after received a grant of a thousand pounds per annum in compensation for her loss of Phœnix Park.

concluded by hoping she might live to see him hanged. The duke heard her with the uttermost calmness, and when she had exhausted her abusive vocabulary, quietly replied, 'Madam, I am not in so much haste to put an end to your days; for all I wish with regard to you is, that I may live to see you grow old.' And, bowing low, the fine old soldier left her presence. It may be added, though the duke was deprived of the lord lieutenancy, the countess's pious wish regarding him was never fulfilled.

It now occurred to those who had relentlessly persecuted the chancellor, that though they were safe as long as Charles reigned, his death would certainly place them in peril. For they sufficiently knew the Duke of York's character to be aware when he ascended the throne he would certainly avenge the wrongs suffered by his father-in-law. Accordingly these men, prominent amongst whom were the Duke of Buckingham, Sir Thomas Clifford, Lords Arlington, Lauderdale, and Ashley, and Baptist May, resolved to devise means which would prevent the Duke of York ever attaining the power of sovereignty. Therefore scarce a year had gone by since Lord Clarendon's downfall, ere rumours were spread abroad that his majesty was about to put away the queen. This was to be effected, it was said, by the king's acknowledgment of a previous marriage with Lucy Walters, mother of the Duke of Monmouth, or by obtaining a divorce on ground of her majesty's barrenness.

The Duke of Buckingham, who was prime mover in this plot, aware of the king's pride in, and fondness for, the Duke of Monmouth, favoured the scheme of his majesty's admission of a marriage previous to that which united him with Catherine of Braganza. And according to Burnet, Buckingham undertook to procure witnesses who would swear they had been present at the ceremony which united him with the abandoned Lucy Walters. Moreover, the Earl of Carlisle, who likewise favoured the contrivance, offered to bring this subject before the House of Lords. However, the king would not consent to trifle with the succession in this vile manner, and the idea was promptly abandoned. But though the project was unsuccessful, it was subsequently the cause of many evils; for the chances of sovereignty, flashing before the eyes of the Duke of Monmouth, dazzled him with hopes, in striving to realize which, he, during the succeeding reign, steeped the country in civil warfare, and lost his head.

The king's friends, ever active for evil, now sought other methods by which he might rid himself of the woman who loved him well, and therefore be enabled to marry again, when, it was trusted, he would have heirs to the crown. It was suggested his union might, through lack of some formality, be proved illegal; but as this could not be effected without open violation of truth and justice, it was likewise forsaken. The Duke of Buckingham now besought his majesty that he would order a bill to divorce himself from the queen to be brought into the House of Commons. The king gave his consent to the suggestion, and the affair proceeded so far that a date was fixed upon for the motion. However, three days previous, Charles called Baptist May aside, and told him the matter must be discontinued.

But even yet my Lord Buckingham did not despair of gaining his wishes. And, being qualified by his character for the commission of abominable deeds, and fitted by his experience for undertaking adventurous schemes, he proposed to his majesty, as Burnet states, that he would give him leave to abduct the queen, and send her out of the kingdom to a plantation, where she should be well and carefully looked to, but never heard of more. Then it could be given out she had deserted him, upon which grounds he might readily obtain a divorce. But the king, though he permitted such a proposal to be made him, contemplated it with horror, declaring 'it was a wicked thing to make a poor lady miserable only because she was his wife, and had no children by him, which was no fault of hers.'

Ultimately these various schemes resolved themselves into a proposition which Charles sanctioned. This was that the queen's confessor should persuade her to leave the world, and embrace a religious life. Whether this suggestion was ever made to her majesty is unknown, for the Countess of Castlemaine, hearing of these schemes, and foreseeing she would be the first sacrificed to a new queen's jealousy, opposed them with such vigour that they fell to the ground and were heard of no more. The fact was, the king took no active part in these designs, not being anxious, now the Duchess of Richmond had accepted his love, to unite himself with another wife. Whilst her grace had been unmarried, the idea had indeed occurred to him of seeking a divorce that he might be free to lay his crown at the feet of the maid of honour. And with such a view in mind he had consulted Dr. Sheldon, Archbishop of Canterbury, as to whether the Church of England 'would allow of a divorce, when both parties were consenting, and one of them lay under a natural incapacity of having children.' Before answering a question on which so much depended, the archbishop requested time for consideration, which, with many injunctions to secrecy, was allowed him. 'But,' says Lord Dartmouth, who vouches for truth of this statement, 'the Duke of Richmond's clandestine marriage, before he had given an answer, made the king suspect he had revealed the secret to Clarendon, whose creature Sheldon was known to be; and this was the true secret of Clarendon's disgrace.' For the king, believing the chancellor had aided the duke in his secret marriage, in order to prevent his majesty's union with Miss Stuart, and the presumable exclusion of the Duke and Duchess of York and their children from the throne, never forgave him.

Though the subject of the royal divorce was no longer mentioned, the disturbances springing from it were far from ended; for the Duke of Buckingham, incensed at Lady Castlemaine's interference, openly quarrelled with her, abused her roundly, and swore he would remove the king from her power. To this end he therefore employed his talents, and with such tact and assiduity that he ultimately fulfilled his menaces. The first step he took towards accomplishing his desires, was to introduce two players to his majesty, named respectively Moll Davis and Nell Gwynn.

The former, a member of the Duke of York's troupe of performers, could boast of goodly lineage, though not of legitimate birth, her father being Thomas Howard, first Earl of Berkshire. She had, early in the year 1667, made her first appearance at the playhouse, and had by her comely face and shapely figure challenged the admiration of the town. Her winsome ways, pleasant voice, and graceful dancing soon made her a favourite with the courtiers, who voted her an excellent wench; though some of her own sex, judging harshly of her, as is their wont towards each other, declared her 'the most impertinent slut in the world.'

Now the Duke of Buckingham knowing her well, it seemed to him no woman was more suited to fulfil his purpose of thwarting the countess; for if he succeeded in awaking the king's passion for the comedian, such a proceeding would not only arouse my lady's jealousy, but likewise humble her pride. Therefore when this court Mephistopheles accompanied his majesty to the playhouse, he was careful to dwell on Moll Davis's various charms, the excellency of her shape, the beauty of her face, the piquancy of her manner. And so impressed was the monarch by Buckingham's descriptions of her, that he soon became susceptible to her fascinations. The amour once begun was speedily pursued; and she was soon enabled to boast, in presence of the players, that the king—whose generosity was great to fallen women — had given her a ring valued at seven hundred pounds, and was about to take, and furnish most richly, a house in Suffolk Street for her benefit and abode. Pepys heard this news in the first month of the year 1668; and soon afterwards a further rumour reached him that she was veritably the king's mistress, 'even to the scorn of the world.'

This intrigue affected Lady Castlemaine in a manner which the Duke of Buckingham had not expected. Whilst sitting beside Charles in the playhouse, she noticed his attention was riveted upon her rival, when she became melancholy and out of humour to a vast degree, in which condition she remained some days. But presently rallying her spirits, she soon found means to divert her mind and avenge her wrongs, of which more shall be recorded hereafter. Meanwhile, the poor queen, whose feelings neither the king nor his courtiers took into consideration, bore this fresh insult with such patience as she could summon to her aid, on one occasion only protesting against her husband's connection with the player. This happened when the Duke of York's troupe performed in Whitehall the tragedy of 'Horace,' 'written by the virtuous Mrs. Phillips.' The courtiers assembled on this occasion presented a brilliant and goodly sight. Evelyn tells us 'the excessive gallantry of the ladies was infinite, those [jewels] especially on Lady Castlemaine esteemed at forty thousand pounds and more, far outshining ye queene.' Between each act of the tragedy a masque and antique dance was performed. When Moll Davis appeared, her majesty, turning pale from sickness of heart, and trembling from indignation at the glaring insult thrust upon her, arose and left the apartment boisterous with revelry, where she had sat a solitary sad figure in its midst. As a result of her intimacy with the king, Moll Davis bore him a daughter, who subsequently became Lady Derwentwater. But the Duke of Buckingham's revenge upon my Lady Castlemaine was yet but half complete; and therefore whilst the monarch carried on his intrigue with Moll Davis, his grace, enlarging upon the wit and excellency of Nell Gwynn, besought his majesty to send for her. This request the king complied with readily enough, and she was accordingly soon added to the list of his mistresses. Nell Gwynn, who was at this period in her eighteenth year, had joined the company of players at the king's house, about the same time as Moll Davis had united her fortunes with the Duke of York's comedians. Her time upon the stage was, however, but of brief duration; for my Lord Buckhurst, afterwards Earl of Dorset, a witty and licentious man, falling in love with her, induced her to become his mistress, quit the theatre, and forsake the society of her lover, Charles Hart, a famous actor and great-nephew of William Shakespeare. And she complying with his desires in these matters, he made her an allowance of one hundred pounds a year, on which she returned her parts to the manager, and declared she would act no more.

Accordingly in the month of July, 1667, she was living at Epsom with my Lord Buckhurst and his witty friend Sir Charles Sedley, and a right merry house they kept for a time. But alas, ere the summer had died there came a day when charming Nell and his fickle lordship were friends no more, and parting from him, she was obliged to revert to the playhouse again.

Now Nell Gwynn being not only a pretty woman, but moreover an excellent actress, her return was welcomed by the town. Her achievements in light comedy were especially excellent, and declared entertaining to a rare degree. Pepys, who witnessed her acting 'a comical part' in the 'Maiden Queen,' a play by Dryden, says he could 'never hope to see the like done again by man or woman. So great performance of a comical part,' he continues, 'was never, I believe, in the world before as Nell do this, both as a mad girle, then most and best of all when she comes in like a young gallant; and hath the motions and carriage of a spark the most that ever I saw any man have. It makes me, I confess, admire her.' In the part of Valeria, in 'Tyrannic Love,' she was also pronounced inimitable; especially in her delivery of the epilogue. The vein of comedy with which she delivered the opening lines, addressed to those about to bear her dead body from the stage, was merry beyond belief. 'Hold!' she cried out to one of them, as she suddenly started to life—

> 'Hold! are you mad? you damned confounded dog!
> I am to rise and speak the epilogue.'

Before the year 1667 ended, she had several times visited his majesty at Whitehall. The king was now no less assured of her charms as a woman, than he had previously been convinced of her excellence as an actress. In due time, her intimacy with the monarch resulted in the birth of two sons; the elder of which was created Duke of St. Albans, from whom is descended the family now bearing that title: the second died young and unmarried.

Through influence of these women, my Lady Castlemaine's power over the king rapidly diminished, and at last ceased to exist; seeing which, as Burnet says, 'She abandoned herself to great disorders; one of which by the artifice of the Duke of Buckingham was discovered by the king in person, the party concerned leaping out of the window.' The gallant to whom the worthy bishop refers was John Churchill, afterwards the great Duke of Marlborough, at this time a handsome stripling of eighteen summers. In his office as page to the Duke of York, he frequently came under notice of her ladyship, who, pleased with the charms of his boyish face and graceful figure, intimated his love would not prove unacceptable to her. Accordingly he promptly entered into an intrigue with the countess, who, in the first fervour of her affection, presented him with five thousand pounds. With this sum he purchased a life annuity of five hundred pounds, which, as Lord Chesterfield writes, 'became the foundation of his subsequent fortune.' Nor did her generosity end here : at a cost of six thousand crowns she obtained for him the post of groom of the bedchamber to the Duke of York, and was instrumental in subsequently forwarding his advancements in the army.

My Lady Castlemaine was by no means inclined to spend her days in misery because the royal favour was no longer vouchsafed her; and therefore, by way of gratifying her amorous disposition, and satisfying her desires for revenge, conducted intrigues not only with John Churchill and Harry Jermyn, but likewise with one Jacob Hall, a noted acrobat. This man was not only gifted with strength and agility, but likewise with grace and beauty : so that, as Granger tells us, ' The ladies regarded him as a due composition of Hercules and

Adonis.' His dancing on the tight rope at Bartholomew Fair was 'a thing worth seeing and mightily followed;' whilst his deeds of daring at Southwark Fair were no less subjects of admiration and wonder. The countess was so charmed by the performance of this well-proportioned athlete in public, that she became desirous of conversation with him in private; and he was accordingly introduced to her by Beck Marshall, the daughter of a Presbyterian minister, who had become a player. Nor did the rope-dancer on closer acquaintance disappoint the countess, who found his society so entertaining, that she frequently visited him in his lodgings, a compliment he courteously returned. Moreover, she allowed him a yearly salary, and openly showed her admiration for him by having their portraits painted in one picture: in which she is represented playing a fiddle, whilst he leans over her, touching the strings of a guitar.

Her amours in general, and her intimacy with the rope-dancer in particular, becoming common talk of the town, his majesty was much incensed; and it grieved him the more that one who dwelt in his palace, and was yet under his protection, should divide her favours between a king and a mountebank. Accordingly bitter feuds arose between her and the monarch, when words of hatred, scorn, and defiance were freely exchanged. His majesty upbraiding her with a love for the rope-dancer, she replied with much spirit, 'it very ill became him to throw out such reproaches against her: that he had never ceased quarrelling unjustly with her, ever since he had betrayed his own mean low inclinations: that to gratify such a depraved taste as his, he wanted the pitiful strolling actresses whom he had lately introduced into their society.' Then came fresh threats from the lips of this beautiful fury, followed by passionate storms of tears.

The king, who loved ease greatly, and valued peace exceedingly, became desirous of avoiding such harrowing scenes. Accordingly, he resolved to enter into a treaty with his late mistress, by which he would consent to grant her such concessions as she desired, providing she promised to discontinue her intrigues with objectionable persons, and leave him to pursue his ways without reproach. By mutual consent, his majesty and the countess selected the Chevalier de Grammont to conduct this delicate business; he being one in whose tact and judgment they had implicit confidence. After various consultations and due consideration, it was agreed the countess should abandon her amours with Henry Jermyn and Jacob Hall, rail no more against Moll Davis or Nell Gwynn, or any other of his majesty's favourites, in consideration for which Charles would create her a duchess, and give her an additional pension in order to support her fresh honours with becoming dignity.

And as the king found her residence in Whitehall no longer necessary to his happiness, Berkshire House was purchased for her as a suitable dwelling. This great mansion, situated at the south-west corner of St. James's Street, facing St. James's Palace, was surrounded by pleasant gardens devised in the Dutch style, and was in every way a habitation suited for a prince. This handsome gift was followed by a grant of the revenues of the Post Office, amounting to four thousand seven hundred pounds a year, which was at first paid her in weekly instalments. On the 3rd of August, 1670, Barbara, Countess

of Castlemaine, was created Baroness Nonsuch,
of Nonsuch Park, Surrey; Countess of Southampton; and Duchess of Cleveland in the peerage
of England. The reasons for crowding these
honours thick upon her were, as the patent
stated, 'in consideration of her noble descent,
her father's death in the service of the crown,
and by reason of her personal virtues.'

Nor did his majesty's extravagant favours to
her end here. She was now, as Mr. Povy told
his friend Pepys, 'in a higher command over the
king than ever—not as a mistress, for she scorns
him, but as a tyrant, to command him.' In consequence of this power, she was, two months
after her creation as duchess, presented by the
monarch with the favourite hunting seat of
Henry VIII., the magnificent palace and great
park of Nonsuch, in the parishes of Cheam and
Malden, in the county of Surrey. And yet a
year later, she received fresh proofs of his royal
munificence by the gift of 'the manor, hundred,
and advowson of Woking, county Surrey; the
manor and advowson of Chobham, the hundred
of Blackheath and Wootton, the manor of Bagshot (except the park, site of the manor and

manor-house, and the Bailiwick, and the office of the Bailiwick, called Surrey Bailiwick, otherwise Bagshot Bailiwick), and the advowson of Bisley, all in the same county.'

Her wealth, the more notable at a time when the king was in debt, and the nation impoverished from expenditure necessary to warfare, was enormous. Andrew Marvell, writing in August, 1671, states: 'Lord St. John, Sir R. Howard, Sir John Bennet, and Sir W. Bicknell, the brewer, have farmed the customs. They have signed and sealed ten thousand pounds a year more to the Duchess of Cleveland; who has likewise near ten thousand pounds a year out of the new farm of the country excise of Beer and Ale; five thousand pounds a year out of the Post Office; and they say, the reversion of all the King's Leases, the reversion of places all in the Custom House, the green wax, and indeed what not? All promotions spiritual and temporal pass under her cognizance.'

CHAPTER IV.

Louise de Querouaille.—The Triple Alliance.—Louise is created Duchess of Portsmouth.—Her grace and the impudent comedian.—Madam Ellen moves in society.—The young Duke of St. Albans.—Strange story of the Duchess of Mazarine.—Entertaining the wits at Chelsea. Luxurious suppers.—Profligacy and wit.

THE Duchess of Cleveland having shared the fate common to court favourites, her place in the royal affections was speedily filled by a mistress whose influence was even more baneful to the king, and more pernicious to the nation. This woman was Louise de Querouaille, the descendant of a noble family in Lower Brittany. At an early age she had been appointed maid of honour to Henrietta, youngest sister of Charles II., soon after the marriage of that princess, in 1661, with the Duke of Orleans, brother to Louis XIV. Fate decreed that Mademoiselle de Querouaille should be brought into England by means of a political movement; love ordained she should reign mistress of the king's affections.

It happened in January, 1668, that a Triple Alliance had been signed at the Hague, which engaged England, Sweden, and the United Provinces to join in defending Spain against the power of France. A secret treaty in this agreement furthermore bound the allies to check the ambition of Louis XIV., and, if possible, reduce his encroaching sway. That Charles II. should enter into such an alliance was galling to the French monarch, who resolved to detach his kinsman from the compact, and bind him to the interests of France. To effect this desired purpose, which he knew would prove objectionable to the British nation, Louis employed Henrietta, Duchess of Orleans, to visit England on pretext of pleasure and affection, and secretly persuade and bribe her brother to the measures required.

The young duchess, though an English princess, had at heart the interests of the country in which she had been reared, and which on her marriage she had adopted as her own. She therefore gladly undertook this mission, confident of her success from the fact that of all his family she had ever been the most tenderly beloved by Charles. Therefore she set out from France, and in the month of May, 1670, arrived at Dover, to which port the king, queen, and court hastened, that they might greet and entertain her. For full ten days in this merry month, high revelry was held at Dover, during which time Henrietta skilfully and secretly effected the object of her visit. And her delight was now the greater, inasmuch as one item which this agreement entrusted her to make, engaged that Charles would, as soon as he could with safety, follow the example of his brother the Duke of York, and become a Catholic. In carrying out this purpose Louis promised him substantial aid and sure protection. Likewise, it may be mentioned, did the French king engage to grant him a subsidy equal to a million a year, if Charles joined him in an attack on Holland.

The prospect of his sister's return filled the king with sorrow, which increased as the term of her visit drew to an end. 'He wept when he parted with her,' wrote Monsieur Col-

DUCHESS OF PORTSMOUTH.

bert, the French ambassador, who significantly adds, 'whatever favour she asked of him was granted.'

Now Louis, knowing the weakness of the English monarch's character, and aware of his susceptibility to female loveliness, had despatched Mademoiselle de Querouaille in the train of Henrietta. Satisfied that Charles could not resist her charms, the French monarch had instructed this accomplished woman, who was trusted in his councils, to accept the royal love, which it was surmised would be proffered her; so that by the influence which she would consequently obtain, she might hold him to the promises he might make the Duchess of Orleans.

As had been anticipated, the king became enamoured of this charming woman, who, before departing with the princess, faithfully promised to return and become his mistress. In his desire to possess her the merry monarch was upheld by his grace of Buckingham, who, continuing in enmity with the Duchess of Cleveland, resolved to prevent her regaining influence over the king by adding the beautiful Frenchwoman to the number of his mistresses. He therefore told Charles, in the sarcastic manner it was occasionally his wont to use, 'it was a decent piece of tenderness for his sister to take care of some of her servants;' whilst on being sent into France, he assured Louis 'he could never reckon himself sure of the king, but by giving him a mistress that should be true to his interests.' But neither king required urging to a resolution on which both had separately determined; and soon Mademoiselle Querouaille was ready for her journey to England. A yacht was therefore sent to Dieppe to convey her, and presently she was received at Whitehall by the lord treasurer, and her arrival celebrated in verse by Dryden. Moreover, that she might have apartments in the palace, the king at once appointed her a maid of honour to her majesty, this being the first of a series of favours she was subsequently to receive. Evelyn, writing in the following October, says it was universally reported a ceremonious espousal, devoid of the religious rite, had taken place between his majesty and Mademoiselle Querouaille at Lord Arlington's house at Euston. 'I acknowledge,' says this trustworthy chronicler, 'she was for the most part in her undresse all day, and that there was fondnesse and toying with that young wanton; nay, 'twas said I was at the former ceremony, but 'tis utterly false; I neither saw nor heard of any such thing whilst I was there, tho' I had ben in her chamber, and all over that apartment late enough, and was myself observing all passages with much curiosity.'

She now became a central figure in the brilliant court of the merry monarch, being loved by the king, flattered by the wits, and tolerated by the queen, to whom—unlike the Duchess of Cleveland—she generally paid the greatest respect. Her card tables were thronged by courtiers eager to squander large sums for the honour of playing with the reigning sultana; her suppers were attended by wits and gallants as merry and amorous as those who had once crowded round my Lady Castlemaine in the zenith of her power. No expense was too great for his majesty to lavish upon her; no honour too high with which to reward her affection. The authority just mentioned says her apartments at Whitehall were luxuriously furnished 'with ten times the richnesse and glory beyond the Queene's; such massy pieces of plate, whole tables and stands of incredible value.' After a residence of little more than three years at court she was raised by King Charles to the peerage as Baroness of Petersfield, Countess of Farnham, and Duchess of Portsmouth; whilst the French king, as a mark of appreciation for the services she rendered France, conferred upon her the Duchy of Aubigny, in the province of Berri in France, to which he added the title and dignity of Duchess and Peeress of France, with the revenues of the territory of Aubigny. And two years later King Charles, prodigal of the honours he conferred upon her, ennobled the son she had borne him in 1672. The titles of the Duke of Richmond and Lennox having lately reverted to the crown by the death of Frances Stuart's husband, who was last of his line, the bastard son of the French mistress was created Duke of Richmond and Earl of March in England, and Duke of Lennox and Earl of Darnley in Scotland. To these proud titles the present head of the noble house of Richmond and Lennox—by virtue of the grant made by Louis XIV. to his ancestress—likewise adds that of Duc d'Aubigny in the peerage of France.

But though honoured by the king, and flattered by the court, the Duchess of Portsmouth was far from enjoying uninterrupted happiness; inasmuch as her peace was frequently disturbed by jealousy. The principal cause of her uneasiness during the first five years of her reign was the king's continued infatuation for Nell Gwynn; now, by reason of the elevated position she enjoyed, styled Madam Ellen. This 'impudent comedian,' as Evelyn calls her, was treated by his majesty with extreme indulgence and royal liberality. In proof of the latter statement, it may be mentioned that in less than four years from the date of her first becoming his mistress, he had wantonly lavished sixty thousand pounds upon her, as Burnet affirms. Moreover, he had purchased as a town mansion for her 'the first good house on the left-hand side of St. James's Square, entering Pall Mall,' now the site of the Army and Navy Club; had given her likewise a residence situated close by the Castle at Windsor; and a summer villa located in what was then the charming village of Chelsea. To such substantial gifts as these he added the honour of an appointment at court: when the merry player was made one of the ladies of the privy chamber to the queen. Samuel Pegg states this fact, not generally known, and assures us he discovered it 'from the book in the lord chamberlain's office.'

From her position as the king's mistress, Madam Ellen moved on terms of perfect equality with the Duchess of Portsmouth's friends—supping with my Lady Orrery, visiting my Lord Cavendish, and establishing a friendship with the gay Duchess of Norfolk. This was a source of deep vexation to the haughty Frenchwoman; but Nell Gwynn's familiarity with the king was a cause of even greater mortification. Sir George Etherege records in verse when the monarch was 'dumpish' Nell would 'chuck the royal chin;' and it is stated that, mindful of her former conquests over Charles Hart and Charles Lord Buckley, it was her habit to playfully style his majesty 'Charles the Third.' Her wilfulness, wit, and beauty enabled her to maintain such a strong hold upon the king's heart, that he shared his time equally between her and the Duchess of

Portsmouth. Indignant that a woman from the playhouse should receive such evidences of the royal affection, her grace lost no opportunity of insulting Nell, who responded by mimicry and grimaces, which threw those who witnessed the comedy into fits of laughter, and covered the wrathful duchess with confusion.

But though the light-hearted actress frequently treated disdain with ridicule, she could occasionally analyze the respective positions held by herself and the duchess with seriousness. Madame de Sévigné tells us, Nell would reason in this manner : ' This duchess pretends to be a person of quality ; she affirms she is related to the best families in France, and when any person of distinction dies she puts herself in mourning. If she be a lady of such quality, why does she demean herself to be a courtesan ? She ought to die with shame. As for me, it is my profession. I do not pretend to anything better. The king entertains me, and I am constant to him at present. He has a son by me ; I contend that he ought to acknowledge him—and I am well assured that he will, for he loves me as well as the duchess.'

To have her son ennobled, and by this means raise him to an equality with the offspring of her grace, became the desire of Nell Gwynn's life. To her request that this favour might be granted, the king had promised compliance from time to time, but had as frequently postponed the fulfilment of his word. At last, weary of beseeching him, she devised a speech which she trusted might have the desired effect. Accordingly, when the monarch came to see her one day, he found her in a pensive mood, playing with her pretty boy; and the lad, being presently set upon his feet, he promptly tottered down the room, whereon she cried out to him, 'Come here, you little bastard!' Hearing this word of evil import applied to his son, the monarch begged she would not use the expression. 'I am sorry,' said she regretfully, 'but, alas, I have no other name to give him!' His majesty took the hint, and soon after bestowed on him that of Charles Beauclerk, and created him Baron of Heddington, in Oxon, and Earl of Burford in the same county; and finally, when he had reached the age of ten years, raised him to the dignity of Duke of St. Albans.

After a reign of five years in the court of the merry monarch, her Grace of Portsmouth was destined to encounter a far more formidable rival than Nell Gwynn, in the person of the Duchess of Mazarine. This lady, on her arrival in England in 1675, possessed most of the charms which had rendered her notable in youth. To the attraction they lent was added an interest arising from her personal history, in which King Charles had once figured, and to which fate had subsequently added many pages of romance.

Hortensia Mancini, afterwards Duchess of Mazarine, was descendant of a noble Roman family, and niece of the great Julius Mazarine, cardinal of the church, and prime minister of France. Her parents dying whilst she, her sister and brother were young, they had been reared under the care of his eminence. According to the memoirs of the duchess, the cardinal's peace must have frequently been put to flight by his charges, whose conduct, he declared, exhibited neither piety nor honour. Mindful of this, he placed his nieces under the immediate supervision of Madame de Venelle, who was directed to have the closest guard over them. A story related by the duchess shows in what manner this lady's duty was carried out, and what unexpected results attended it on one occasion.

When the court visited Lyons, in the year 1658, the cardinal's nieces and their governess lodged in a commodious mansion in one of the public squares. 'Our chamber windows, which opened towards the market-place,' writes Hortensia, ' were low enough for one to get in with ease. Madame de Venelle was so used to her trade of watching us, that she rose even in her sleep to see what we were doing. One night, as my sister lay asleep with her mouth open, Madame de Venelle, after her accustomed manner, coming, asleep as she was, to grope in the dark, happened to thrust her finger into her mouth so far that my sister, starting out of her sleep, made her teeth almost meet in her finger. Judge you the amazement they both were in to find themselves in this posture when they were thoroughly awake. My sister was in a grievous fret. The story was told the king the next day, and the court had the divertisement of laughing at it.'

Whilst the great minister's nieces were yet extremely young, Louis XIV. fell passionately in love with the elder, Maria, and his marriage with her was frustrated only by the united endeavours of the queen mother and the cardinal. A proposal to raise Hortensia to the nominal dignity of queen was soon after made on behalf of Charles II., who sought her as his bride. But he being at the time an exile, banished from his kingdom, and with little hope of regaining his throne, the offer was rejected by Cardinal Mazarine as unworthy of his favourite niece.

His eminence was, however, anxious to see her married, and accordingly sought amongst the nobility of France a husband suitable to her merits and equal to her condition, she being not only a beautiful woman but, through his bounty, the richest heiress in Christendom. It happened the cardinal's choice settled upon one who had fallen in love with Hortensia, and who had declared, with amorous enthusiasm, that if he had but the happiness of being married to her, it would not grieve him to die three months afterwards.

This young noble was Armand Charles de la Porte, Duke de Meilleraye, who had the sole recommendation of being one of the richest peers of France. On condition that he and his heirs should assume the name of Mazarine and arms of that house, the cardinal consented to his becoming the husband of his niece. And the great minister's days rapidly approaching their end, the ceremony was performed which made Hortensia, then at the age of thirteen, Duchess of Mazarine. A few months later the great cardinal expired, leaving her the sum of one million six hundred and twenty-five thousand pounds sterling. Alas that she should have died in poverty, and that her body should have been seized for debt!

Scarce had the first weeks of her married life passed away, when the young wife found herself mated to one wholly unsuited to her character. She was beautiful, witty, and frivolous; he jealous, dull, and morose. The incompatibility of their dispositions became as discernible to him, as they had become intolerable to her; and, as if to avenge the fate which had united them, he lost no opportunity of thwarting her desires, by such means striving to bend her lissom quality to the gnarled shape of his unhappy nature.

With such a purpose in view, no opportunity was neglected to curb her pleasures or oppose her inclinations. He continually forced her to leave Paris, and even when her condition required rest and care, compelled her to accompany him on long and weary journeys, undertaken by him in consequence of his diplomatic missions. If she received two successive visits from one man, he was instantly forbidden the house. If she called her carriage, the coachman received orders not to obey. If she betrayed a preference for one maid more than another, the favourite was instantly dismissed. Moreover, the duchess was surrounded by spies, her movements being rigorously watched, and invariably reported. Nor would the duke vouchsafe an explanation to his young wife regarding the cause of this severe treatment, but continued the even course of such conduct without intermission or abatement.

After displaying these eccentricities for some years, they suddenly associated themselves with religion, when he became a fanatic. Her condition was now less endurable than before; his whims more ludicrous and exasperating. With solemnity he declared no one could in conscience visit the theatre; that it was a sin to play blind man's buff, and a heinous crime to retire to bed late. And presently, his fanaticism increasing, he prohibited the woman who nursed his infant to suckle it on Fridays or Saturdays; that instead of imbibing milk, it might, in its earliest life, become accustomed to fasting and mortification of the flesh.

The young duchess grew hopeless of peace. All day her ears were beset by harangues setting forth her wickedness, by exhortations calling her to repentance, and by descriptions of visions vouchsafed him. By night her condition was rendered scarcely less miserable. 'No sooner,' says St. Evremond, 'were her eyes closed, than Monsieur Mazarine (who had the devil always present in his black imagination) wakes his best beloved, to make her partaker—you will never be able to guess of what—to make her partaker of his nocturnal visions. Flambeaux are lighted, and search is made everywhere; but no spectre does Madame Mazarine find, except that which lay by her in the bed.'

The distresses to which she was subjected

were increased by a knowledge that her husband was squandering her vast fortune. In what manner the money was spent she does not state. 'If,' she writes, 'Monsieur Mazarine had only taken delight in overwhelming me with sadness and grief, and in exposing my health and my life to his most unreasonable caprice, and in making me pass the best of my days in an unparalleled slavery, since heaven had been pleased to make him my master, I should have endeavoured to allay and qualify my misfortunes by my sighs and tears. But when I saw that by his incredible dilapidations and profuseness, my son, who might have been the richest gentleman in France, was in danger of being the poorest, there was no resisting the force of nature; and motherly love carried it over all other considerations of duty, or the moderation I proposed to myself. I saw every day vast sums go away: moveables of inestimable prices, offices, and all the rich remains of my uncle's fortune, the fruits of his labours, and the rewards of his services. I saw as much sold as came to three millions, before I took any public notice of it; and I had hardly anything left me of value but my jewels, when Monsieur Mazarine took occasion to seize upon them.'

She therefore sought the king's interference, but as the duke had interest at court, she received but little satisfaction. Then commenced disputes, which, after months of wrangling, ended by the duchess escaping in male attire out of France, in company with a gay young cavalier, Monsieur de Rohan. After various wanderings through Italy, and many adventures in Savoy, she determined on journeying to England. That her visit was not without a political motive, we gather from St. Evremond; who, referring to the ascendency which the Duchess of Portsmouth had gained over his majesty, and the uses she made of her power for the interests of France, tells us, ' The advocates for liberty, being excluded from posts and the management of affairs, contrived several ways to free their country from that infamous commerce; but finding them ineffectual, they at last concluded that there was no other course to take than to work the Duchess of Portsmouth out of the king's favour, by setting up against her a rival who should be in their interest. The

Duchess of Mazarine was thought very fit for their purpose, for she outshined the other both in wit and beauty.'

Charles de St. Denis, Seigneur de St. Evremond, was a soldier, philosopher, and courtier, who had distinguished himself by his bravery, learning, and politeness. Having fallen under the displeasure of the French court, he had, in the year 1662, sought refuge in England, where he had been welcomed with the courtesy due to his rank, and the esteem which befitted his merits. Settling in the capital, he mixed freely in the companionship of wits, gallants, and courtiers who constituted its society; and delighted with London as a residence, he determined on making England his country by adoption. An old friend and fervent admirer of the Duchess of Mazarine, he had received the news of her visit with joy, and celebrated her arrival in verse.

The reputation of her loveliness and the history of her life having preceded her, the court became anxious to behold her; the king, mindful of the relationship he had once sought with the duchess, grew impatient to welcome her. After a few days' rest, necessary to remedy the fatigue of her journey, she appeared at Whitehall. By reason of her beauty, now ripened rather than impaired by time, and those graces which attracted the more from the fascination they had formerly exercised, she at once gained the susceptible heart of the monarch. St. Evremond tells us her person 'contained nothing that was not too lovely.' In the 'Character of the Duchess of Mazarine,' which he drew soon after her arrival in London, he has presented a portrait of her worth examining, not only for sake of the object it paints, but for the quaint workmanship it contains. 'An ill-natured curiosity,' he writes, 'makes me scrutinize every feature in her face, with a design either to meet there some shocking irregularity, or some disgusting disagreeableness. But how unluckily do I succeed in my design. Every feature about her has a particular beauty, that does not in the least yield to that of her eyes, which, by the consent of all the world, are the finest in the universe. One thing there is that entirely confounds me: her teeth, her lips, her mouth, and all the graces that attend it, are lost amongst the great variety of beauties in her face; and what is but indifferent in her, will not suffer us to consider what is most remarkable in others. The malice of my curiosity does not stop here. I proceed to spy out some defect in her shape; and I find I know not what graces of nature so happily and so liberally scattered in her person, that the genteelness of others only seems to be constraint and affectation.'

The king—to whom the presence of a beautiful woman was as sunshine to the earth—at once offered her his affections, the gallants tendered their homage, the ladies of the court volunteered the flattery embodied in imitation. And by way of practically proving his admiration, his majesty graciously allotted her a pension of four thousand pounds a year, with apartments in St. James's Palace.

The sovereignty which the Duchess of Portsmouth had held for five years over the monarch's heart was now in danger of downfall; and probably would have ended, but for Madame Mazarine's indiscretions. It happened a few months after her arrival in London, the Prince of Monaco visited the capital. Young in years, handsome in person, and extravagant in expenditure, he dazzled the fairest women at court; none of whom had so much power to please him in all as the Duchess of Mazarine. Notwithstanding the king's generosity, she accepted the prince's admiration; and resolved to risk the influence she had gained, that she might freely love where she pleased. Her entertainment of a passion, as sudden in development as fervid in intensity, enraged the king; but his fury served only to increase her infatuation, seeing which, his majesty suspended payment of her pension.

The gay Prince of Monaco in due time ending his visit to London, and leaving the Duchess of Mazarine behind him, she, through the interposition of her friends, obtained his majesty's pardon, was received into favour, and again allowed her pension.

She now ruled, not only mistress of the king's heart, but queen of a brilliant circle of wits and men of parts, whose delight it became to heed the epigrams and eccentricities which fell from her lips. Her rooms at St. James's, and her house in Chelsea, became the rendezvous of the most polite and brilliant society in England. In the afternoons, seated amongst her monkeys, dogs, parrots, and pets, she discoursed on philosophy, love, religion, politics, and plays; whilst at night her saloons were thrown open to such as delighted in gambling. Then the duchess, seated at the head of the table, her dark eyes flashing with excitement, her red lips parted in expectation, followed the fortunes of the night with anxiety: all compliments being suspended and all fine speeches withheld the while, nought being heard but the rustle of cards and the chink of gold.

Dainty and luxurious suppers followed, when rare wines flowed, and wit long suppressed found joyous vent. Here sat Charles beside his beautiful mistress, happy in the enjoyment of the present, careless of the needs of his people; and close beside him my Lord of Buckingham, watchful of his majesty's face, hatching dark plots whilst he turned deft compliments. There likewise were my Lord Dorset, the easiest and wittiest man living; Sir Charles Sedley, one learned in intrigue; Baptist May, the monarch's favourite; Tom Killigrew, who jested on life's follies whilst he enjoyed them; the Countess of Shrewsbury, beautiful and amorous; and Madam Ellen, who was ready to mimic or sing, dance or act, for his majesty's diversion.

And so, whilst a new day stole upon the world without, tapers burned low within the duchess's apartments; and the king, his mistress, and a brave and gallant company ate, drank, and made merry.

NELL GWYN.

CHAPTER V.

A storm threatens the kingdom.—The Duke of York is touched in his conscience.—His interview with Father Simons.—The king declares his mind.—The Duchess of York becomes a catholic.—The circumstances of her death.—The Test Act introduced.—Agitation of the nation.—The Duke of York marries again.—Lord Shaftesbury's schemes.—The Duke of Monmouth.—William of Orange and the Princess Mary.—Their marriage and departure from England.

WHILST the surface life of the merry monarch sped onward in its careless course, watchful eyes took heed of potent signs boding storms and strife. The storm which shook the kingdom to its centre came anon; the strife which dethroned a monarch was reserved for the succeeding reign. These were not effected by the king's profligacy, indolence, or extravagance, but because of a change in the religious belief of the heir-apparent to the crown.

The cloud, no bigger than a man's hand, which presently spread and overcast the political horizon, was first observed towards the beginning of the year 1669. The Rev. J. S. Clarke, historiographer to George III., chaplain to the royal household, and librarian to the Prince Regent, in his 'Life of James II., collected out of Memoirs writ of his own hand,' tells us that about this time the Duke of York 'was sensibly touched in his conscience, and began to think seriously of his salvation.' Accordingly, the historian states, 'he sent for one Father Simons, a Jesuit, who had the reputation of a very learned man, to discourse with him upon that subject; and when he came, he told him the good intentions he had of being a catholic, and treated with him concerning his being reconciled to the church. After much discourse about the matter, the Jesuit very sincerely told him, that unless he would quit the communion of the Church of England, he could not be received into the Catholic Church. The duke then said he thought it might be done by a dispensation from the pope, alleging the singularity of his case, and the advantage it might bring to the catholic religion in general, and in particular to those of it in England, if he might have such dispensation for outwardly appearing a protestant, at least till he could own himself publicly to be a catholic, with more security to his own person and advantage to them. But the father insisted that even the pope himself had not the power to grant it, for it was an unalterable doctrine of the Catholic Church, not to do ill that good might follow. What this Jesuit thus said was afterwards confirmed to the duke by the pope himself, to whom he wrote upon the same subject. Till this time his royal highness believed (as it is commonly believed, or at least said by the Church of England doctors) that dispensations in any such cases are by the pope easily granted; but Father Simons's words, and the letter of his holiness, made the duke think it high time to use all the endeavours he could, to be at liberty to declare himself, and not to live in so unsafe and so uneasy a condition.'

Inasmuch as what immediately followed touches a point of great delicacy and vast importance, the words of the historian, mainly taken from the 'Stuart Papers,' are best given here. 'His royal highness well-knowing that the king was of the same mind, and that his majesty had opened himself upon it to Lord Arundel of Wardour, Lord Arlington, and Sir Thomas Clifford, took an occasion to discourse with him upon that subject about the same time, and found him resolved as to his being a catholic, and that he intended to have a private meeting with those persons above named at the duke's closet, to advise with them about the ways and methods fit to be taken for advancing the catholic religion in his dominions, being resolved not to live any longer in the constraint he was under. The meeting was on the 25th of January. When they were met according to the king's appointment, he declared his mind to them on the matter of religion, and said how uneasy it was to him not to profess the faith he believed; and that he had called them together to have their advice about the ways and methods fittest to be taken for the settling of the catholic religion in his kingdoms, and to consider of the time most proper to declare himself, telling them withal that no time ought to be lost; that he was to expect to meet with many and great difficulties in bringing it about, and that he chose rather to undertake it now, when he and his brother were in their full strength and able to undergo any fatigue, than to delay it till they were grown older and less fit to go through with so great a design. This he spoke with great earnestness, and even with tears in his eyes; and added, that they were to go about it as wise men and good catholics ought to do. The consultation lasted long, and the result was, that there was no better way for doing this work than to do it in conjunction with France, and with the assistance of his Most Christian majesty.' Accordingly, the secret treaty with France was entered into, as already mentioned.

No further movement towards professing the catholic religion was made by the king or his brother for some time. The tendencies of the latter becoming suspected, his actions were observed with vigilance, when it was noted, that although he attended service as usual with the king, he no longer received the sacrament. It was also remarked the Duchess of York, whose custom it had been to communicate once a month, soon followed his example. Her neglect of this duty was considered the more conspicuous as she had been bred a staunch protestant, and ever appeared zealous in her support of that religion. Moreover, it was noted that, from the beginning of the year 1670, she was wont to defend the catholic faith from such errors as it had been charged withal.

These matters becoming subjects of conversation at court, soon reached the ears of Bishop Morley, who had acted as her confessor since her twelfth year, confession being then much practised in the English Church. Thereon he hastened to her, and spoke at length of the inferences which were drawn from her neglect of receiving the sacrament, in answer to which she pleaded business and ill-health as sufficient excuses. But he, suspecting other causes, gave her advice, and requested she would send for him in case doubts arose in her mind concerning the faith she professed. Being now free from all uncertainties, she readily promised compliance with his desire, and added, 'No priest had ever taken the confidence to speak to her on those matters.'

The fact that she no longer communicated

becoming more noticed as time passed, the king spoke to his brother concerning the omission, when the duke told him she had become a catholic. Hearing this, Charles requested him to keep her change of faith a secret, which was accordingly done, none being aware of the act but Father Hunt, a Franciscan friar, Lady Cranmer, one of her women of the bedchamber, and Mr. Dupuy, servant to the duke. In a paper she drew up relative to her adoption of the catholic religion, preserved in the fifth volume of the 'Harleian Miscellany,' she professes being one of the greatest enemies that faith ever had. She likewise declares no man or woman had said anything, or used the least persuasion to make her change her religion. That had been effected, she adds, by a perusal of Dr. Heylin's 'History of the Reformation;' after which she spoke severally to Dr. Sheldon, Archbishop of Canterbury, and Dr. Blandford, Bishop of Worcester, who told her 'there were many things in the Roman Church which it was very much to be wished they had kept—as confession, which was no doubt commanded by God; and praying for the dead, which was one of the ancient things in Christianity—that for their parts they did it daily, though they would not own to it.'

The duchess pondered over what she had read and heard, and being a woman accustomed to judge for herself, and act upon her decisions, she, in the month of August, 1670, became a member of the Catholic Church, in which communion she died seven months later. For fifteen months previous to her demise she had been suffering from a complication of diseases, with which the medical skill of that day was unable to cope, and these accumulating, in March, 1671, ended her days. The 'Stuart Papers' furnish an interesting account of her death. Seeing the hour was at hand which would sever her from all earthly ties, she besought her husband not to leave her whilst life remained. She likewise requested that in case Dr. Blandford or any other of the bishops should come to visit her, he would tell them she had become a member of the Catholic Church; but if they insisted on seeing her she was satisfied to admit them, providing they would not distress her by arguments or controversy.

Soon after she had expressed these desires, Bishop Blandford arrived and begged permission to see her, hearing which the duke went into the drawing-room, where his lordship waited, and delivered the message with which the duchess had charged him. Thereon the bishop said, 'he made no doubt but that she would do well since she was fully convinced, and had not changed out of any worldly end.' He then went into the room, and having made 'a short Christian exhortation suitable to the condition she was in,' took his departure. Presently the queen came and sat by the dying woman, with whom she had borne many wrongs in common; and later on, the Franciscan friar being admitted, the duchess 'received all the last sacraments of the Catholick Church, and dyed with great devotion and resignation.'

Though no mystery was now made concerning the faith in which she died, the duke, from motives of prudence, continued to preserve the secret of his having embraced the same religion. He still publicly attended service on Sundays with the king, but continued to absent himself from communion. At last, the Christmastide of the year 1672 being at hand, his majesty besought Lord Arundel and Sir Thomas (now Lord) Clifford to persuade the duke to take the sacrament with him, 'and make him sensible of the prejudice it would do to both of them should he forbear so to do, by giving the world so much reason to believe he was a catholick.' To this request these honest gentlemen replied it would be difficult to move the duke to his majesty's desires; but even if they succeeded, it would fail to convince the world his royal highness was not a catholic. With these answers Charles seemed satisfied; but again on Christmas Eve he urged Lord Clifford to advise the duke to publicly communicate on the morrow. His royal highness, not being so unscrupulous as the king, refused compliance with his wishes.

The following Easter he likewise refrained from communicating. Evelyn tells us that 'a most crowded auditorie' had assembled in the chapel royal on this Sunday; possibly it had been drawn there to hear the eloquence of Dr. Sparrow, Bishop of Exeter—probably to observe the movements of the king's brother. 'I staied to see,' writes Evelyn, 'whether, according to costome, the Duke of York received the communion with the king ; but he did not, to the amazement of everybody. This being the second year he had forborn and put it off, and within a day of the parliament sitting, who had lately made so severe an act against ye increase of poperie, gave exceeding griefe and scandal to the whole nation, that the heyre of it, and ye sonn of a martyr for ye Protestant religion, should apostatize. What the consequence of this will be God only knows, and wise men dread.'

That the nation might no longer remain in uncertainty concerning the change the duke was suspected to have made, a bill, commonly called the 'Test Act,' was, at the instigation of Lord Shaftesbury, introduced into the House of Commons, on its reassembling. In substance this set forth, that all persons holding office, or place of trust, or profit, should take the oaths of supremacy and allegiance in a public court; receive the sacrament according to the Church of England in some parish church on the Lord's Day; and deliver a certificate of having so received communion, signed by the respective ministers and churchwardens, and proved by two credible witnesses on oath. After prolonged debates upon this singular bill, it was passed through both houses of parliament, and received a reluctant consent from the king.*

A great commotion followed the passing of this act. Immediately the Duke of York resigned his post of lord high admiral of England. Suspicion now became certainty: he was truly a papist. His enemies were elated with triumph, his friends dejected by regret. Before public feeling had time to subside, it was thoroughly startled by the news that Lord Clifford, who was supposed to be a staunch protestant, had delivered up his staff of office as lord treasurer; and Lord Bellasis and Sir Thomas Strickland, papists both, 'though otherwise men of quality and ability,' had relinquished their places at court. The king was perplexed, the parliament divided into factions, the nation disturbed. No man knew who might next proclaim himself a papist. As days passed, excitement increased; for hundreds who held positions in the army, or under the crown—many

* This act continued in force until the reign of George IV.

of whom had fought for the king and his father—by tendering their resignations, now proved themselves slaves of what a vigorous writer calls the 'Romish yoke: such a thing,' he adds, 'as cannot, but for want of a name to express it, be called a religion.'

Public agitation steadily rose. Evelyn tells us, 'he dare not write all the strange talk of the town.' Distrust of the king, fear of his brother, hatred of popery and papists, filled men's minds and blinded their reason with prejudice. That the city had seven years ago been destroyed by fire, in accordance with a scheme of the wicked Jesuits, was a belief which once more revived: the story of the gunpowder plot was again detailed. Fearful suspicions sprang up and held possession of the vulgar mind, that the persecutions suffered by protestants in the days of Queen Mary might be repeated in the reign of the present monarch, or of his brother. That heaven might defend the country from being overrun by popery, the House of Commons besought his majesty to order a day of fasting and humiliation. And by way of adding fury to the gathering tempest, the bishops, as Burnet states, 'charged the clergy to preach against popery, which alarmed the court as well as the city, and the whole nation.'

The king therefore complained to Dr. Sheldon, Archbishop of Canterbury, that the discourse heard in every pulpit throughout the capital and the kingdom was 'calculated to inflame the people, and alienate them from him and his government.' Upon which Dr. Sheldon called the bishops together, that he might consult with them as to what answer he had best make. Whereon these wise men declared 'since the king himself professed the protestant religion, it would be a thing without a precedent that he should forbid his clergy to preach in defence of a religion, while he himself said he was of it.' The next action which served to inflame public prejudice against catholicism, was the marriage of the Duke of York to a princess professing that faith.

Soon after the death of his wife, it was considered wise and well his royal highness should marry again. Of the four sons and four daughters the duchess had borne him, three sons and one daughter had died before their mother, and the surviving son and another daughter quickly followed her to the tomb: therefore, out of eight children but two survived, Mary and Anne, at this time respectively aged nine and seven. It being desirable there should be a male heir-presumptive to the crown, the king was anxious his brother should take unto himself a second wife. And that a lady might be found worthy of the exalted station to which such a union would raise her, the Earl of Peterborough was sent incognito to report on the manners and appearance of the princesses of the courts of Neuburg and of Modena. Not being impressed by the merits of those belonging to the former, he betook himself to the latter, where, seeing the young Princess d'Este, then in her fifteenth year, he came to the conclusion no better choice could be made on behalf of the duke than this fair lady. On communicating this opinion to his royal highness and to his majesty, the king commissioned him to demand the hand of the princess in marriage for his brother.

Difficulties regarding this desired union now arose. The young lady, having been bred in great simplicity and ignorance, had never heard of such a country as England, or such a person as the Duke of York; and therefore had no mind to adventure herself in a distant land, or wed a man of whom she knew nought. Moreover, she had betrayed an inclination to spend her days in the seclusion of a convent, and had no thought of marriage. Her mother, the Duchess of Modena, then regent, by reason of her husband's death and her son's minority, was anxious for so advantageous an alliance. And being unable to gain her daughter's consent, she sought the interference of the pope, who wrote to the young princess, that compliance with her mother's request would 'most conduce to the service of God and the public good.' On this, Mary Beatrice Eleonora, Princess d'Este, daughter of the fourth Duke of Modena, consented to become Duchess of York. Whereon the Earl of Peterborough made a public entry into Modena, as ambassador extraordinary of Charles II.; and having agreed to all the articles of marriage, wedded her by proxy for the royal duke.

Meanwhile, news that the heir to the crown was about to wed a papist spread with rapidity throughout the kingdom, carrying alarm in its course. If sons were born of the union, they would, it was believed, undoubtedly be reared in the religion of their parents, and England in time become subject to a catholic king. The possibility of such a fate was to the public mind fraught with horror; and the House of Commons, after some angry debates on the subject, presented an address to the king, requesting he would abandon this proposed marriage. To this he was not inclined to listen, his honour being so far involved in the business; but notwithstanding his unwillingness, his councillors urged him to this step, and prayed he would stop the princess, then journeying through France on her way to England. This so incensed him that he immediately prorogued parliament, and freed himself from further interference on the subject.

On the 21st of November, 1673, the future duchess landed at Dover, where the duke awaited her, attended by a scant retinue. For the recent protestations, made in the House of Commons against the marriage, having the effect of scaring the courtiers, few of the nobility, and but one of the bishops, Dr. Crew of Oxford, ventured to accompany him, or greet his bride. On the day of her arrival the marriage was celebrated, 'according to the usual form in cases of the like nature.' The 'Stuart Papers' give a brief account of the ceremony. 'The Duke and Duchess of York, with the Duchess of Modena her mother, being together in a room where all the company was present, as also my Lord Peterborough, the bishop asked the Duchess of Modena and the Earl of Peterborough whether the said earl had married the Duchess of York as proxy of the duke? which they both affirming, the bishop then declared it was a lawful marriage.'

This unpopular union served to strengthen the gathering storm; protests against popery were universally heard; an article in the marriage settlement, which guaranteed the duchess a public chapel, was broken; and the duke was advised by Lord Berkshire to retire into the country, 'where he might hunt and pray without offence to any or disquiet to himself.' This counsel he refused to heed. Until his majesty should command him to the contrary, he said, he would always attend upon him, and do such service as he thought his duty and the king's security required of him. His enemies became more wrathful at this reply, more suspicious of popery, and more fearful of his influence with the king. They therefore sought to have him removed from his majesty's councils and presence by act of parliament.

Consequently, when both Houses assembled on the 7th of January, 1674, the lords presented an address to the monarch, praying he would graciously issue a proclamation, requiring all papists, or reputed papists, within five miles of London, Westminster, or Southwark, to depart ten miles from these respective cities, and not return during this session of Parliament. A few days afterwards an act was introduced into the House of Commons proposing a second test, impossible for catholics to accept, the refusal of which would not only render them incapable of holding any office, civil or military, or of sitting in either House of Parliament, but 'of coming within five miles of the court.' This unjust bill, to which, if it passed both houses, Charles dared not refuse assent, threw the court and country into a state of renewed excitement. Knowing it was a blow levelled at the duke, his friends gathered round him, determined to oppose it by might and main; and after great exertions caused a clause to be inserted excepting his royal highness from the test. This was ultimately carried by a majority of two votes, which, says Clarke, 'put the little Earl of Shaftesbury so out of humour, that he said he did not care what became of the bill, having that proviso in it.'

This noble earl, who was chief among the royal duke's enemies, was a prominent figure in the political history of the time. Dr. Burnet tells us his lordship's strength lay in the knowledge of England, and of all considerable men. 'He understood,' says the bishop, 'the size of their understandings and their tempers; and he knew how to apply himself to them so dexterously, that though by his changing sides so often it was very visible how little he was to be depended on, yet he was to the last much trusted by all the discontented party. He had no regard to truth or justice.' As rich in resources as he was poor in honour, he renewed a plan for depriving the Duke of York from succession to the crown; which, though it had failed when formerly attempted, he trusted might now succeed. This was to declare the Duke of Monmouth the king's legitimate son and heir to the throne of England, a scheme which the ambitious son of Lucy Walters was eager to forward.

His majesty's affection for him had strengthened with time, and his favours had been multiplied by years. On the death of the Duke of Albemarle, Captain General of the Forces, Monmouth had been appointed to that high office; and some time later had been made General of the Kingdom of Scotland, posts of greatest importance. Relying on the monarch's love and the people's admiration for this illegitimate scion of royalty, Lord Shaftesbury hoped to place him on the throne. As the first step necessary in this direction was to gain his majesty's avowal of a union with Lucy Walters, he ventured on broaching the subject to the king; at which Charles was so enraged that he declared, 'much as he loved the Duke of Monmouth, he had rather see him hanged at Tyburn than own him as his legitimate son.' There was, however, another man engaged in a like design to the noble earl, who, if not less scrupulous, was more daring.

This was one Ross, a Scotsman, who had

been made governor of the young duke on his first coming into England, and who had since acted as his friend and confidant. Now Ross, who had not failed to whisper ambitious thoughts into his pupil's head, at this time sought Dr. Cosin, Bishop of Durham, and, according to the 'Stuart Papers,' told him ' he might do a great piece of service to the Church of England in keeping out popery, if he would but sign a certificate of the king's marriage to the Duke of Monmouth's mother, with whom that bishop was acquainted in Paris. Ross also told the bishop, to make the thing more easy to him, that during his life the certificate should not be produced or made use of.' The same papers state that, as a bishop's certificate is a legal proof of marriage, Dr. Cosin's compliance would have been invaluable to the duke and his friends. His lordship, however, rejected the proposition, and laid the matter before the king, who expelled Ross from court.

Horror of popery and fear of a papist sovereign increased with time, care having been taken by my Lord Shaftesbury and his party that the public mind, once inflamed, should be kept ignited. For this purpose he spread reports abroad that the Irish were about to rise in rebellion, backed by the French; and that the papists in London had entered into a vile conspiracy to put their fellow citizens to the sword on the first favourable opportunity. To give this latter statement a flavour of reality he, assuming an air of fright, betook himself one night to the city, and sought refuge in the house of a fanatic, in order, he said, that he might escape the catholics, who had planned to cut his throat.

A tempest, dark and dangerous, was gathering fast, which the court felt powerless to subdue. The king's assurance to parliament that 'he would endeavour to satisfy the world of his steadfastness for the security of the protestant religion,' had little avail in soothing the people. Many of them suspected him to be a catholic at heart; others knew he had accepted the bounty of a country feared and detested by the nation. Deeds, not words, could alone dispel the clouds of prejudice which came between him and his subjects; and accordingly he set about the performance of such acts as might bring reconciliation in their train.

The first of these was the confirmation, according to the Protestant Church, of the Lady Mary, eldest daughter of the Duke of York, and after him heir presumptive to the crown ; the second and more important was the marriage of that princess to William of Orange. This prince was son of the king's eldest sister, and therefore grandson of Charles I. As a hero who, by virtue of his statesmanship and indomitable courage, had rescued Holland from the hateful power of France, he was regarded not only as the saviour of his country, but as the protector of protestantism. Already a large section of the English nation turned their eyes towards him as one whom they might elect some day to wield the sceptre of Great Britain. Subtle, ambitious, and determined, a silent student of humanity, a grave observer of politics, a sagacious leader in warfare, he had likewise begun to look forward towards the chances of succeeding his uncle in the government of England—in hopes of which he had been strengthened by the private overtures made him by Shaftesbury, and sustained by the public prejudices exhibited against the Duke of York.

The proposed union between him and the heiress presumptive to the crown was regarded by the nation with satisfaction, and by the prince as an act strongly favouring the realization of his desires for sovereignty. Cold and grave in temperament, sickly and repulsive in appearance, blunt and graceless in manner, he was by no means an ideal bridegroom for a fair princess; but neither she nor her father had any choice given them in a concern so important to the pacification of the nation. She, it was whispered at court, had previously given her heart to a brave young Scottish laird; and her father, it was known, had already taken an instinctive dislike to the man destined to usurp his throne. In October, 1677, the Prince of Orange came to England, ostensibly to consult with King Charles regarding the establishment of peace between France and the Confederates; but the chief motive of his visit was to promote his marriage, which had some time before been proposed, and owing to political causes had been coolly received by him. Now, however, his anxiety for the union was made plain to the king, who quickly agreed to his desires.

'Nephew,' said he to the sturdy Dutchman, 'it is not good for man to be alone, and I will give you a help meet for you; and so,' continues Burnet, 'he told him he would bestow his niece on him.'

The same afternoon the monarch informed his council that 'the Prince of Orange, desiring a more strict alliance with England by marriage with the Lady Mary, he had consented to it, as a thing he looked on as very proper to unite the family, and which he believed would be agreeable to his people, and show them the care he had of religion, for which reason he thought it the best alliance he could make.' When his majesty had concluded this speech, the Duke of York stepped forward, and declared his consent to the marriage. He hoped 'he had now given a sufficient testimony of his right intentions for the public good, and that people would no more say he designed altering the government in church or state; for, whatever his opinion on religion might be, all that he desired was, that men might not be molested merely for conscience' sake.'

The duke then dined at Whitehall with the

king, the Prince of Orange, and a noble company; after which he returned to St. James's, where he then resided. Dr. Edward Luke, at this time tutor to the Lady Mary, and subsequently Archdeacon of Exeter, in his interesting manuscript diary, informs us that on reaching the palace, the duke, with great tenderness and fatherly affection, took his daughter aside, 'and told her of the marriage designed between her and the Prince of Orange; whereupon her highness wept all that afternoon and the following day.' Her tears had not ceased to flow when, two days after the announcement of her marriage, Lord Chancellor Finch, on behalf of the council, came to congratulate her; and Lord Chief Justice Rainsford, on the part of the judges, complimented her in extravagant terms.

This union, which the bride regarded with so much repugnance, was appointed to take place on the 4th of November, that date being the bridegroom's birthday, as likewise the anniversary of his mother's nativity. Dr. Luke gives a quaint account of the ceremony. 'At nine o'clock at night,' he writes, 'the marriage was solemnized in her highness's bedchamber. The king, who gave her away, was very pleasant all the while; for he desired that the Bishop of London would make haste lest his sister [the Duchess of York] should be delivered of a son, and so the marriage be disappointed. And when the prince endowed her with all his worldly goods [laying gold and silver on the book], he willed to put all up in her pockett, for 'twas clear gains. At eleven o'clock they went to bed, when his majesty came and drew the curtains, saying, "Hey! St. George for England!"'

For a time both court and town seemed to forget the trouble and strife which beset them. Bonfires blazed in the streets, bells rang from church towers, the populace cheered lustily; whilst at Whitehall there were many brilliant entertainments. These terminated with a magnificent ball, held on the 15th instant, the queen's birthday; at the conclusion of this festivity the bride and bridegroom were to embark in their yacht, which was to set sail next morning for Holland. For this ball the princess had 'attired herself very richly with all her jewels;' but her whole appearance betrayed a sadness she could not suppress in the present, and which the future did not promise to dispel. For already the bridegroom, whom the maids of honour had dubbed the 'Dutch monster' and 'Caliban,' had commenced to reveal glimpses of his unhandsome character; 'and the court began to whisper of his sullennesse or clownishnesse, that he took no notice of his princess at the playe and balle, nor came to see her at St. James', the day preceding that designed for their departure.'

The wind being easterly, they were detained in England until the 19th, when, accompanied by the king, the Duke of York, and several persons of quality, they went in barges from Whitehall to Greenwich. The princess was sorely grieved, and wept unceasingly. When her tutor 'kneeled down and kissed her gown' at parting, she could not find words to speak, but turned her back that she might hide her tears; and, later on, when the queen ' would have comforted her with the consideration of her own condition when she came into England, and had never till then seen the king, her highness replied, "But, madam, you came into England; but I am going out of England."'

CHAPTER VI.

The threatened storm bursts.—History of Titus Oates and Dr. Tonge.—A dark scheme concocted.—The king is warned of danger.—The narrative of a horrid plot laid before the treasurer.—Forged letters.—Titus Oates before the council.—His blunders.—A mysterious murder.—Terror of the citizens.—Lord Shaftesbury's schemes.—Papists are banished from the capital.—Catholic peers committed to the Tower.—Oates is encouraged.

THE marriage of the Lady Mary, though agreeable to the public mind, by no means served to distract it from the turmoil by which it was beset. Hatred of catholicism, fear of the Duke of York, and distrust of the king, disturbed the nation to its core. Rumours were now noised abroad, which were not without foundation, that the monarch and his brother had renewed the treaty with France, by which Louis engaged to send troops into England to support Charles, when the latter saw fit to lay aside duplicity, and proclaim himself a catholic. And, notwithstanding the rigorous Test Acts, it was believed many high positions at court were held by those who were papists at heart. Occasion was therefore ripe for the invention of a monstrous fraud, the history of which has been transmitted under the title of the Popish Plot.

The chief contrivers of this imposture were Titus Oates and Dr. Tonge. The first of these was son of a ribbon-weaver, who, catching the fanatical spirit of the Cromwellian period, had ranted as an Anabaptist preacher. Dissent, however, losing favour under the restoration, Oates, floating with the current of the times, resolved to become a clergyman of the Church of England. He therefore took orders at Cambridge, officiated as curate in various parishes, and served as chaplain on board a man-of-war. The time he laboured as spiritual shepherd to his respective flocks was necessarily brief; for his grossly immoral practices becoming notable, he was in every case ousted from his charge. The odium attached to his name was moreover increased by the fact, that his evidence in two cases of malicious prosecution had been proved false; for which he had been tried as a perjurer. Deprived of his chaplaincy for a revolting act of profligacy, driven from congregations he had scandalized, homeless and destitute, he in an evil hour betook himself to Dr. Ezrael Tonge, to whom he had long been known, and besought compassion and relief.

The Rev. Dr. Tonge, rector of St. Michael's, Wood Street, was a confirmed fanatic and political alarmist. For some years previous to this time, he had published quarterly treatises dealing with such wicked designs of the Jesuits as his heated brain devised. These he had printed and freely circulated, in order, as he acknowledged, 'to arouse and awaken his majesty and the parliament' to a sense of danger. He had begun life as a gardener, but left that honest occupation that he might cultivate flowers of rhetoric for the benefit of Cromwell's soldiers. Like Titus Oates, he had become suddenly converted to orthodox principles on return of the king, and had, through interest, obtained the rectorship of St. Michael's. Bishop Burnet considered him 'a very mean divine, (who) seemed credulous and simple, and was full of projects and notions.'

Another historian who lived in those days, the Rev. Laurence Eachard, Archdeacon of Stowe, states Dr. Tonge was 'a man of letters, and had a prolific head filled with all the Romish plots and conspiracies since the reformation.' According to this author, Tonge took Oates into his house, provided him with lodging, diet, and clothes; and when the latter complained he knew not where to get bread, the rector told him 'he would put him in a way.' After this, finding Oates a man of great ingenuity and cunning, 'he persuaded him,' says Archdeacon Eachard, 'to insinuate himself among the papists, and get particular acquaintance with them; which being effected, he let him understand that there had been several plots in England to bring in popery, and that if he would go beyond sea among the Jesuits, and strictly observe their ways, it was possible there might be one at present; and if he could make that out, it would be his preferment for ever; but, however, if he could get their names, and some information from the papists, it would be very easy to rouse people with the fears of popery.'

Hungering for gold, and thirsting for notoriety, Oates quickly agreed to the scheme laid before him. Accordingly he became acquainted with, and was received into the Catholic Church by, Father Berry, a Jesuit, and in May, 1677, was sent by the Jesuits to study in one of their seminaries, situated in Valladolid, in Spain. Oates, however, though he had proved himself an excellent actor, could not overcome his evil propensities, and before seven months had passed, he was expelled from the monastery.

Returning to England, he sought out Dr. Tonge, to whom he was unable to recount the secret of a single plot. Confident, however, that wicked schemes against the lives and properties of innocent protestants were being concocted by wily Jesuits, the fanatical divine urged Oates to present himself once more before them, bewail his misconduct, promise amendment, and seek readmission to their midst. Following his advice, Oates was again received by the Jesuits, and sent to their famous seminary at St. Omer's; where, though he had reached the age of thirty years, he was entered among the junior students. For six months he remained here, until his vices becoming noted, he was turned away in disgrace. Again he presented himself before the rector of St. Michael's, knowing as little of popish plots as he did on his previous return. But Tonge, though disappointed, was not disheartened; if no scheme existed, he would invent one which should startle the public, and save the nation. Such proposals as he made towards the accomplishment of this end were readily assented to by Oates, in whose breast wounded pride and bitter hate rankled deep. Therefore, after many consultations they resolved to draw up a 'Narrative of a Horrid Plot.' This was repeatedly changed and enlarged, until eventually it assumed the definite shape of a deposition, consisting of forty-three distinct articles, written with great formality and care, and embodying many shocking and criminal charges.

The narrative declared that in April, 1677, the deponent was employed to carry letters from the Jesuits in London to members of their order in Spain; these he broke open on the journey, and discovered that certain Jesuits had been sent into Scotland to encourage the presbyterians to rebel. Arrived in Valladolid, he heard one

Armstrong, in a sermon delivered to students, charge his majesty with most foul and black-mouthed scandals, and use such irreverent, base expressions as no good subjects could repeat without horror. He then returned to England, and was soon after sent to St. Omer with fresh letters, in which was mentioned a design to stab or poison his majesty— Père la Chaise, the French king's confessor, having placed ten thousand pounds at the disposal of the Jesuits that they might, by laying out such a sum, the more successfully accomplish this deed. While abroad the deponent had read many letters, relating to the execution of Charles II., the subverting of the present government, and the establishment of the Romish religion. Returning again to England, he became privy to a treaty with Sir George Wakeman, the queen's physician, to poison the king; and likewise with an agreement to shoot him, made between the Jesuits and two men, named Honest William and Pickering. He had heard a Jesuit preach a sermon to twelve persons of quality in disguise, in which he asserted 'that protestants and other heretical princes were *ipso facto* deposed because such; and that it was as lawful to destroy them as Oliver Cromwell or any other usurper.' He also became aware that the dreadful fire had been managed by Strange, the provincial of the Jesuits, who employed eighty-six men in distributing seven hundred fire-balls to destroy the city; and that notwithstanding his vast expenses, he gained fourteen thousand pounds by plunder carried on during the general confusion, a box of jewels, consisting of a thousand carat weight of diamonds, being included in the robbery.

The document containing these remarkable statements was finished in August, 1678. It now remained to have it brought before the king or the council. Tonge was resolved this should be done in a manner best calculated to heighten the effect of their narrative; at the same time he was careful to guard the fact that he and Oates had an intimate knowledge of each other. Not knowing anyone of interest at court, he sought out Christopher Kirby, a man employed in the king's laboratory, of whom he had some slight knowledge, and, pledging him to the strictest secrecy, showed him the 'Narrative of the Horrid

Plot,' and besought his help in bringing it under the notice of his majesty in as private a manner as possible.

This aid was freely promised ; and next day, the date being the 13th of August, when the monarch was about to take his usual airing in the park, Kirby drew near, and in a mysterious tone bade his majesty take care, for his enemies had a design against his life, which might be put into execution at any moment. Startled by such words, the king asked him in what manner was it intended his life should be taken ; to which he replied, 'It might be by pistol ; but that to give a more particular account of the matter, required greater privacy.' The monarch, who quickly recovered his first surprise, resolved to take his usual exercise ; and, subduing his curiosity, he bade Kirby attend him on his return from the park, and tell him what he knew of the subject.

When the time arrived, Kirby saw his majesty alone, and related to him in brief that two men waited but an opportunity to shoot him ; and Sir George Wakeham had been hired to poison him ; which news, he concluded, had been imparted to him by a worthy man living close at hand, who would attend his majesty's pleasure when that was manifested.

Bewildered by such intelligence, yet suspicious of its veracity, the king ordered Kirby to summon his informant that evening by eight o'clock. When that hour came his majesty repaired to the Red Room, and there met Dr. Tonge, who delivered his narrative into his hands. The rector was convinced the great moment he had so long awaited, in which he would behold the monarch aroused to a sense of his danger, had arrived. He was doomed to bitter disappointment. His majesty coolly took the narrative, and without opening it, said it should be examined into. On this Tonge begged it might be kept safe and secret, 'lest the full discovery should otherwise be prevented and his life endangered.' The monarch replied that, before starting with the court to-morrow for Windsor, he would place it in the hands of one he could trust, and who would answer for its safety. He then bade him attend on the Lord Treasurer Danby next morning.

In obedience to this command, Tonge waited

on his lordship at the appointed time, and by the character of his replies helped to develop his story of the plot. When asked if the document he had given his majesty was the original of the deponent, Tonge admitted it was in his own handwriting. On this, Lord Danby expressed a desire to see the original, and likewise become acquainted with its author. Nothing abashed, the rector replied the manuscript was in his house, and accounted for its possession by stating that, singularly enough, it had been thrust under his door—he did not know by whom, but fancied it must be by one who, some time before, had discussed with him on the subject of this conspiracy. Whereon his lordship asked him if he knew the man, and was answered he did not, but he had seen him lately two or three times in the streets, and it was likely he should see him soon again.

Being next questioned as to whether he had any knowledge of Honest William, or Pickering, the villains who sought the king's life, he answered he had not. Immediately, however, he remembered it was their habit to walk in St. James's Park, and said, if any man was appointed to keep him company, he was almost certain he would have opportunities of letting that person see these abominable wretches. Finally, Lord Danby asked him if he knew where they dwelt, for it was his duty to have them arrested at once ; but of their abode Tonge was completely ignorant, though he was hopeful he should speedily be able to obtain the required information.

He was therefore dismissed, somewhat to his satisfaction, being unprepared for such particular examination; but in a couple of days he returned to the charge, determined his tale should not be discredited for lack of effrontery. On this occasion he said he had met the man he suspected of being author of the document, who owned himself as such, and stated that his name was Titus Oates, but requested Tonge would keep it a strict secret, 'because the papists would murder him if they knew what he was doing.' Moreover, Oates had given him a second paper full of fresh horrors concerning this most foul plot. Taking this with him, the lord treasurer hastened to Windsor, that he might consult the king. having first left a servant with Tonge, in hopes the latter might catch sight of Honest William and Pickering in their daily walk through the park, and have them arrested. On Danby recounting Tonge's statements to the king, his majesty was more convinced than before the narrative was wholly without foundation, and refused to make it known to his council or the Duke of York. Therefore the lord-treasurer, on conclusion of a brief visit, left Windsor for his country residence, situated at Wimbledon.

For some days no fresh disclosure was made concerning this horrid plot, until late one night, when Dr. Tonge arrived in great haste at Lord Danby's house, and informed him some of the intended regicides had resolved on journeying to Windsor next morning, determined to assassinate the king. He added, it was in his power to arrange that the earl's servant should ride with them in their coach, or at least accompany them on horseback, and so give due notice of their arrival, in order that they might be timely arrested. Alarmed by this intelligence, Danby at once hastened to Windsor, and informed the king of what had come to his knowledge. Both endured great suspense that night, and next day their excitement was raised to an inordinate pitch by seeing the earl's servant ride towards the castle with all possible speed. When, however, the man was brought into his majesty's presence, he merely delivered a message from Dr. Tonge, stating the villains 'had been prevented from taking their intended journey that day, but they proposed riding to Windsor next day, or within two days at farthest.' Before that time had arrived, another message came to say, ' one of their horses being slipped in the shoulder, their trip to Windsor was postponed.'

Taking these foolish excuses, as well as Dr. Tonge's prevaricating answers and mysterious statements, into consideration, the king was now convinced the ' Narrative of a Horrid Plot ' was an invention of a fanatic or a rogue. He was, therefore, desirous of letting the subject drop into obscurity; but Lord Danby, foreseeing in the sensation which its avowal would create, a welcome cloud to screen the defects of his policy, which parliament intended to denounce, urged his majesty to lay the matter before his privy council. This advice the king refused to accept, saying, ' he should alarm all England, and put thoughts of killing him into people's heads, who had no such ideas before.' Somewhat disappointed, the lord treasurer returned once more to Wimbledon, the king remaining at Windsor, and no further news of the plot disturbed the even tenour of their lives for three days.

At the end of that time Dr. Tonge, now conscious of the false steps he had taken, conceived a fresh scheme by which his story might obtain credence, and he gain wealth and fame. Accordingly he wrote to Danby, informing him a packet of letters, written by the Jesuits and concerning the plot, would, on a certain date, be sent to Mr. Bedingfield, chaplain to the Duchess of York. Such information was most acceptable to Danby at the moment; he at once started for Windsor, and laid this fresh information before the king. To his lordship's intense surprise, his majesty handed him the letters. These, five in number, containing treasonable expressions and references to the plot, had been some hours before handed by Mr. Bedingfield to the Duke of York, saying, he 'feared some ill was intended him by the same packet, because the letters therein seemed to be of a dangerous nature, and that he was sure they were not the handwriting of the persons whose names were subscribed to the letters.' On examination, they were proved to be most flagrant forgeries. Written in a feigned hand, and signed by different names, they were evidently the production of one man; the same want of punctuation, style of expression, and peculiarities of spelling being notable in all. The Duke of York, foreseeing malice was meant by them, forcibly persuaded the king to place the epistles before the privy council. Accordingly, they were handed to Sir William Jones, attorney general, and Sir Robert Southwell, who stated, upon comparing them with Dr. Tonge's narrative, they were convinced both were written by the same hand.

Meanwhile, Tonge and Oates, aware of the coldness and doubt with which his majesty had received the 'Narrative of the Horrid Plot,' and ignorant of the fact he had placed the letters before his privy council, resolved to make their story public to the world. It therefore happened on the 6th of September they presented themselves before Sir Edmondbury Godfrey, a justice of the peace, in the parish of St. Martin's, who, not without considerable persuasion, consented to receive a sworn testimony from Titus Oates regarding the truth of his narrative, which had now grown from forty-three to eighty-one articles. This action prevented further secrecy concerning the so-called plot.

A few days later the court returned to town for the winter, when the Duke of York besought the privy council to investigate the strange charges made in the declaration. Accordingly, on the 28th of the month, Tonge and Oates were summoned before it, when the latter, making many additions to his narrative, solemnly affirmed its truth. Aghast at so horrible a relation, the council knew not what to credit. The evil reputation Oates had borne, the baseness of character he revealed in detailing his actions as a spy, the mysterious manner in which the fanatical Tonge accounted for his possession of the document, tended to make many doubt; whilst others, believing no man would have the hardihood to bring forward such charges without being able to sustain them by proof, contended it was their duty to sift them to the end. Believing if he had been entrusted with secret letters and documents of importance, he would naturally retain some of them in order to prove his intended charges, the council asked Oates to produce them; but of these he had not one to show. Nor, he confessed, could he then furnish proof of his words, but promised if he were provided with a guard, and given officers and warrants, he would arrest certain persons concerned in the plot, and seize secret documents such as none could dispute. These being granted him, he immediately caused eight Jesuits to be apprehended and imprisoned. Then he commenced a search for treasonable letters, not only in their houses, but in the homes of such catholics as were noted for their zeal. His investigations were awaited with impatience; nor were they without furnishing some pretext for his accusations.

One of the first dwellings which Titus Oates investigated was that of Edward Coleman. This gentleman, the son of an English divine, had early in life embraced catholicity, for the propagation of which he thenceforth became most zealous. Coming under notice of the court, he became the confidant of the Duke of York, and by him was made secretary to the duchess. A man of great mental activity, religious fervour, and considerable ambition, he had, about four years previous to this time, entered into a correspondence with the confessor of the French king and other Jesuits, regarding the hopes he entertained of Charles II. professing catholicity. Knowing him to be bold in his designs and incautious in his actions, the duke had discharged him from his post as secretary to the duchess, but had retained him in his dependence. This latter circumstance, together with a suspicion of the confidence which had existed between him and his royal highness, prompted Oates to have him arrested, and his house searched. Coleman, having received notice of this design, fled from his home, incautiously leaving behind him some old letters and copies of communications which had passed between him and the Jesuits. These were at once seized, and though not containing one expression which could be construed as treasonable, were, from expectations they set forth of seeing catholicity re-established in England, considered by undiscerning judges, proofs of the statements made by Oates.

On the strength of his discovery, Oates hastened to Sir Edmondbury Godfrey, and swore false informations; becoming aware of which, Coleman, conscious of his innocence, delivered himself up, in hopes of meeting a justice never vouchsafed him.

The privy council now sat morning and evening, in order to examine Oates, whose evidence proved untrustworthy and contradictory to a bewildering degree. When it was pointed out to him the five letters, supposed to come from men of education, contained ill-spelling, bad grammar, and other faults, he, with much effrontery, declared it was a common artifice among the Jesuits to write in that manner, in order to avoid recognition; but inasmuch as real names were attached to the epistles, that argument was not considered just. The subject was not mentioned again. When an agent for these wicked men in Spain, he related, he had been admitted into the presence of Don John, and had seen him counting out large sums of money, with which he intended to reward Sir George Wakeham when he had poisoned the king. Hearing this, his majesty inquired what kind of person Don John was. Oates said he was tall, lean, and black; whereas the monarch knew him to be small, stout, and fair. And on another occasion, when asked where he had heard the French king's confessor hire an assassin to shoot Charles, he replied, 'At the Jesuits' monastery close by the Louvre;' at which the king, losing patience with the impostor, cried out, 'Tush, man! the Jesuits have no house within a mile of the Louvre!' Presently Oates named two catholic peers, Lord Arundel of Wardour and Lord Bellasis, as being concerned in the plot, when the king again spoke to him, saying these lords had served his father faithfully, and fought his wars bravely, and unless proof were clear against them, he would not credit they sought him ill. Then Oates, seeing he had gone too far, said they did not know of the conspiracy, but it had been intended to acquaint them with it in good time. Later on he swore falsely against them.

Meanwhile the wildest sensation was caused by the revelations of this 'hellish plot and attempt to murder the king.' The public mind, long filled with hatred of papacy, was now inflamed to a degree of fury which could only be quenched by the blood of many victims. To the general sensation which obtained, a new terror was promptly added by the occurrence of a supposed horrible and mysterious murder.

On the evening of Saturday, the 12th of October, Sir Edmondbury Godfrey was missing from his home in the parish of St. Martin's. The worthy magistrate was an easy going bachelor of portly appearance, much given to quote legal opinions in his discourse, and to assert the majesty of the law as represented in his person. He was alike respected for his zeal by the protestants, and esteemed for his lenity by the catholics. Bishop Burnet records the worthy knight 'was not apt to search for priests or mass-houses;' and Archdeacon Eachard affirms 'he was well known to be a favourer rather than a prosecutor of the papists.' Accordingly, his disappearance at first begot no evil suspicions; but as he did not return on Monday, his servants became alarmed at the absence of a master whose regularity was proverbial. His brothers were of opinion he was in debt, and sought escape from his creditors; whilst his friends, after their kind, were ready to name certain houses of doubtful repute in which they were certain he had taken temporary lodgings. On his papers being examined, it was found he had set his affairs in order, paid all his debts, and destroyed a quantity of his letters and documents. It was then remembered he had been occasionally susceptible to melancholia —a disease he inherited from his father, who had perished by his own hand. It was noted some days before that on which he was missed, he had appeared listless and depressed. It was known the imprisonment of his friend Coleman had weighed heavily on his spirits. A terrible fear now taking possession of his relatives and friends, thorough search was made for him, which proved vain until the Thursday following his disappearance, when he was accidentally discovered lying in a ditch, a cloth knotted round his neck, and a sword passed through his body, 'at or near a place called Primrose Hill, in the midway between London and Hampstead.'

If he had been murdered, no motive appeared to account for the deed; neither robbery nor revenge could have prompted it. His rings and money, gloves and cane, were found on and near his body; and it was known he had lived in peace with all men. Nor did an inquest lasting two days throw any light upon the mystery. If it were proved he had died by his own hand, the law of that day would not permit his brothers to inherit his property, which was found to be considerable. It was therefore their interest to ignore the fact that strangulation pointed to *felo de se*, and to assume he had been murdered. Accordingly they prohibited the surgeons from opening the body, lest examination should falsify conclusions at which they desired to arrive. A verdict was ultimately returned 'that he was murdered by certain persons unknown to the jurors, and that his death proceeded from suffocation and strangling by a certain piece of linen cloth of no value.'

Occurring at such a moment, his death was at once attributed to the papists, who, it was said, being incensed that the magistrate had received the sworn testimonies of Oates, had sought this bloody revenge. Fear now succeeded bewilderment; desires of vengeance sprang from depths of horror. For two days the mangled remains of the poor knight were exposed to public view, 'and all that saw them went away inflamed.' They were then interred with all the pomp and state befitting one who had fallen a victim to catholicism, a martyr to protestantism. The funeral procession, which took its sad way through the principal throughfares from Bridewell to St. Martin's-in-the-Fields, numbered seventy-two divines, and over twelve hundred persons of quality and consideration. Arriving at the church, Dr. Lloyd, a clergyman remarkable for his fine abhorrence of papists, ascended the pulpit, where, protected by two men of great height and strength, he delivered a discourse, pointing to the conclusion that Sir Edmondbury Godfrey had been sacrificed to the catholic conspiracy, and instigating his hearers to seek revenge. Sir Roger North tells us the crowd in and about the church was prodigious, 'and so heated, that anything called papist, were it cat or dog, had probably gone to pieces in a moment. The catholics all kept close in their houses and lodgings, thinking it a good composition to be safe there.'

The whole city was terror-stricken. 'Men's spirits were so sharpened,' says Burnet, 'that it was looked on as a very great happiness that the people did not vent their fury upon the papists about the town.' Tonge and Oates went abroad protected by body guards, arresting hundreds of catholics; cannon were mounted around Whitehall and St. James's; patrols paraded the streets by day and night; the trained bands were ready to fall in at a moment's notice; preparations were made for barricading the principal thoroughfares; the city gates were kept closed so that admission could be only had through the wickets; and the Houses of Parliament demanded a guard should keep watch on the vaults over which they sat, lest imitators of Guy Fawkes might blow them to pieces. Moreover, it was not alone the safety of the multitude, but the protection of the individual which was sought to be secured. In the dark confusion which general terror produced, each man felt he might be singled out as the next victim of this diabolical plot, and therefore devised means to guard his life from the

hands of murderous papists. North, in his
'Examen,' speaking of this period, tells us:
'There was much recommendation of silk armour,
and the prudence of being provided with it
against the time the protestants were to be
massacred. And, accordingly, there were abundance of those silken back, breast, and headpots
made and sold, that were pretended to be pistol
proof; in which any man dressed up was as safe
as in a house, for it was impossible anyone could
go to strike him for laughing; so ridiculous was
the figure, as they say, of hogs in armour. This
was the armour of defence; but our sparks were
not altogether so tame as to carry their provision
no further, for truly they intended to be assailants upon fair occasion, and had for that
end recommended also to them a certain pocket
weapon, which for its design and efficacy had
the honour to be called a protestant flail. It was
for street and crowd work; and the engine
lurking perdue in a coat pocket, might readily
sally out to execution, and so, by clearing a
great hall, or piazza or so, carry an election
by a choice of polling called knocking down.
The handle resembled a farrier's blood stick, and

the fall was joined to the end by a strong nervous ligature, that in its swing fell just short of the hand, and was made of *lignum vitæ*, or rather, as the poet termed it, *mortis*.'

One day, whilst the town was in this state of consternation, Tonge sent for Dr. Burnet, who hastened to visit him in the apartments allotted him and Oates at Whitehall. The historian says he found Tonge ' so lifted up that he seemed to have lost the little sense he had. Oates came in,' he continues, ' and made me a compliment that I was one that was marked out to be killed. He had before said the same to Stillingfleet of him. But he had made that honour which he did us too cheap, when he said Tonge was to be served in the same manner, because he had translated " The Jesuits' Morals " into English. He broke out into great fury against the Jesuits, and said he would have their blood. But I, to divert him from that strain, asked him what were the arguments that prevailed on him to change his religion and to go over to the Church of Rome? He upon that stood up, and laid his hands on his breast, and said, " God and His holy angels knew that he had never changed, but that he had gone among them on purpose to betray them." This gave me such a character of him, that I could have no regard to anything he said or swore after that.'

The agitation which now beset the public mind had been adroitly fanned into flame by the evil genius of Lord Shaftesbury. Eachard states that if he was not the original contriver of this disturbance, 'he was at least the grand refiner and improver of all the materials. And so much he seemed to acknowledge to a nobleman of his acquaintance, when he said, "I will not say who started the game, but I am sure I had the full hunting of it."' In the general consternation which spread over the land he beheld a means that might help the fulfilment of his strong desires. Chief among these were the exclusion of the Duke of York from the throne, and the realization of his own inordinate ambition. A deist in belief, he abhorred catholicism; a worshipper of self, he longed for power. He had boasted Cromwell had wanted to crown him king, and he narrated to Burnet that a Dutch astrologer had predicted he would yet fill a lofty position. He had long schemed and dreamed, and now it seemed the result of the one and fulfilment of the other were at hand. The pretended discovery of this plot threatened to upheave the established form of government, for the king was one at heart with those about to be brought to trial and death. A quarter of a century had not passed since a bold and determined man had risen up and governed Great Britain. Why should not history repeat itself in this respect? the prospect was alluring. Possessing strong influence, great vanity, and an unscrupulous character, Shaftesbury resolved to stir the nation to its centre, at the expense of peace, honour, and bloodshed.

On the 21st of October, Parliament assembled, when Lord Danby, much against his majesty's inclination, brought the subject of the plot before the Commons. This was a movement much appreciated by the House, which, fired by the general indignation, resolved to deal out vengeance with a strong hand. As befitted such intention, they began by requesting his majesty would order a day of general fasting and prayer, to implore the mercy of Almighty God. The king complying with this desire, they next, 'in consideration of the bloody and traitorous designs,' besought him to issue a proclamation 'commanding all persons being popish recusants, or so reputed,' to depart ten miles from the city. Accordingly, upwards of thirty thousand citizens left London before the 7th of the following month, 'with great lamentations leaving their trades and habitations.' Many of them in a little while secretly returned again. A few days before this latest petition was presented to the monarch, Oates had been examined before the House for over six hours; and so delighted was he by the unprejudiced manner in which his statements were received, that he added several items to them. These were not only interesting in themselves, but implicated peers and persons of quality to the number of twenty-six. The former, including Lords Stafford, Powis, Petre, Bellasis, and Arundel of Wardour, were committed to the Tower, the latter to Newgate prison.

At the end of his examination he was several times asked if he knew more of the plot, or of those concerned with it, to which he emphatically replied he did not. Three days later he remembered a further incident which involved many persons not previously mentioned by him.

Both Houses now sat in the forenoon and afternoon of each day; excitement was not allowed to flag. Oates seldom appeared before the Commons without having fresh revelations to make; but the fertility of his imagination by no means weakened the strength of his evidence in the opinions of his hearers. 'Oates was encouraged,' writes John Evelyn, 'and everything he affirmed taken for gospel.' Indignation against the papists daily increasing in height, the decrees issued regarding them became more rigorous in severity.

On the 2nd of November the king, in obedience to his Parliament, offered a reward of twenty pounds for the discovery of any officer or soldier who, since the passing of the Test Act, 'hath been perverted to the Romish religion, or hears mass.' Two days later a bill was framed 'for more effectually preserving the king's person and government, by disabling papists from sitting in either House of Parliament.' As it was feared a clause would be inserted in this, excluding the Duke of York, the enemies of his royal highness more plainly avowed their object by moving that an address be presented to the king, praying his brother should 'withdraw himself' from his majesty's person and counsels.' This was the first step towards the Bill of Exclusion from Succession which they hoped subsequently to obtain. The monarch, however, determined to check such designs whilst there was yet time; and accordingly made a speech to the peers, in which he said to them, 'Whatever reasonable bills you shall present to be passed into laws, to make you safe in the reign of my successor, so they tend not to impeach the right of succession, nor the descent of the crown in the true line, shall find from me a ready concurrence.'

The intended address was therefore abandoned for the present; but the bill for disabling catholics from sitting in either House of Parliament, having a clause which excepted the Duke of York from that indignity, passed on the 30th of November.

CHAPTER VII.

> Reward for the discovery of murderers.—Bedlow's character and evidence.—His strange story.—Development of the 'horrid plot.'—William Staley is made a victim.—Three Jesuits hung.—Titus Oates pronounced the saviour of his country.—Striving to ruin the queen.—Monstrous story of Bedlow and Oates.—The king protects her majesty.— Five Jesuits executed.—Fresh rumours concerning the papists.—Bill to exclude the Duke of York.—Lord Stafford is tried.—Scene at Tower Hill.—Fate of the conspirators.

BEFORE the remains of Sir Edmondbury Godfrey were laid to rest, a proclamation was issued by the king, offering a reward of five hundred pounds for discovery of the murderers. If one of the assassins betrayed those who helped him in the deed, he should receive, not only the sum mentioned, but likewise a free pardon, and such protection for his security as he could in reason propose. Two days after this had been made public, a man named William Bedlow put himself in communication with Sir William Coventry, Secretary of State, declaring he had a certain knowledge of the murder in question.

Archdeacon Eachard tells us this man 'was one of a base birth and worse manners, who from a poor foot-boy and runner of errands, for a while got into a livery in the Lord Bellasis's family; and having for his villainies suffered hardships and want in many prisons in England, he afterwards turned a kind of post or letter carrier for those who thought fit to employ him beyond sea. By these means he got the names and habitations of men of quality, their relations, correspondents, and interests; and upon this bottom, with a daring boldness, and a dexterous turn of fancy and address, he put himself into the world. He was skilful in all the arts and methods of cheating; but his masterpiece was his personating men of quality, getting credit for watches, coats, and horses; borrowing money, bilking vintners and tradesmen, lying and romancing to the degree of imposing upon any man of good nature. He lived like a wild Arab upon prey, and whether he was in Flanders, France, Spain, or England, he never failed in leaving the name of a notorious cheat and impostor behind him.'

On the 7th of November, Bedlow was brought before the king, and examined by two Secretaries of State. Here he made the extraordinary declaration that he had seen the body of the murdered magistrate lying at Somerset House—then the residence of the queen; that two Jesuits, named La Faire and Walsh, told him they, with the assistance of an attendant in the queen's chapel, had smothered Sir Edmondbury Godfrey between two pillows; that he had been offered two thousand guineas if he would safely remove the body, which on his refusal was carried away, a couple of nights after the murder, by three persons unknown to him, who were servants of the queen's household. Hearing this statement, Sir William Coventry asked him if he knew anything of the popish plot, when he affirmed on oath he was entirely ignorant regarding it; he likewise swore he knew no such man as Titus Oates.

That night he was lodged in Whitehall, in company with Tonge and Oates; and next morning appeared before the House of Lords, when it was evident his memory had wonderfully improved since the previous day. His story now assumed a more concise form. In the beginning of October, he stated, he had been offered the sum of four thousand pounds, to be paid by Lord Bellasis, provided he murdered a man whose name was withheld from him. This he refused. He was then asked to make the acquaintance and watch the movements of Sir Edmondbury Godfrey. With this he complied. Soon after dusk on the 12th of October, the magistrate had been dragged into the court of Somerset House by the Jesuits, and asked if he would send for the documents to which Oates had sworn. On his refusal he had been smothered with a piece of linen cloth; the story of suffocation by pillows, being at variance with the medical evidence, was now abandoned. One of the Jesuits, La Faire, had asked Bedlow to call at Somerset House that night at nine o'clock; and on presenting himself, he was conducted through a gloomy passage into a spacious and sombre room, where a group of figures stood round a body lying on the floor. Advancing to these, La Faire turned the light of a lantern he carried on the face of the prostrate man, when Bedlow recognised Sir Edmondbury Godfrey. He was then offered two thousand guineas if he would remove the body, which was allowed to remain there three days. This he promised to accomplish, but afterwards, his conscience reproving him, he resolved to avoid the assassins; and rather than accept the sum proffered, he had preferred discovering the villainy to the Government.

This improbable story obtained no credit with the king, nor indeed with those whose minds were free from prejudice. 'His majesty,' writes Sir John Reresby, 'told me Bedlow was a rogue, and that he was satisfied he had given false evidence concerning the death of Sir Edmondbury Godfrey.' Many circumstances regarding the narrator and his story showed the viciousness of the one and the falsity of the other. The authority just mentioned states, when Bedlow 'was taxed with having cheated a great many merchants abroad, and gentlemen at home, by personating my Lord Gerard and other men of quality, and by divers other cheats, he made it an argument to be more credited in this matter, saying nobody but a rogue could be employed in such designs.' Concerning the murder, it chanced the king had been at Somerset House visiting the queen, at the time when, according to Bedlow, the deed had been committed. His majesty had been attended by a company of guards, and sentries had been placed at every door; yet not one of them had witnessed a scuffle, or heard a noise. Moreover, on the king sending Bedlow to Somerset House, that he might indicate the apartment in which the magistrate's remains had lain three days, he pointed out a room where the footman waited, and through which the queen's meals were daily carried.

But the dishonesty of his character and falsity of his statements by no means prevented the majority of his hearers from believing, or pretending to believe, his statements; and therefore, encouraged by the ready reception they met, he ventured to make fresh and startling revelations. Heedless of the oath he had taken on the first day of his examination, regarding his ignorance of the popish plot, he now asserted he was well acquainted with all its details. For some four years he had been in the secret employment of the wicked Jesuits, and knew they intended to stab and poison his majesty, establish catholicity in England, and make the pope king. So far, indeed, had their evil machinations been planned, that several popish peers already held commissions for posts they expected to fill in the future. Lord Bellasis and Lord Powis were appointed commanders of the forces in the north and south; whilst Lord Arundel of Wardour had permission to grant such positions as he pleased. Then the Dukes of Buckingham, Ormond, and Monmouth, with Lords Shaftesbury and Ossory, together with many others, were to be murdered by forty thousand papists, who were ready to rise up all over the country at a moment's notice. 'Nor was there,' he added, 'a Roman Catholic of any quality or credit but was acquainted with these designs, and had received the sacrament from their father confessors to be secret in carrying it out.'

It by no means pleased Oates that Bedlow should surpass him in his knowledge of this hellish plot. Therefore, that he might not lose in repute as an informer, he now declared he was also aware of the commissions held by popish peers. He, however, assigned them in a different order. Arundel was to be made chancellor; Powis, treasurer; Bellasis, general of the army; Petre, lieutenant-general; Ratcliffe, major-general; Stafford, paymaster-general; and Langhorn, advocate-general. Nay, his information far outstripped Bedlow's, for he swore that to his knowledge Coleman had given four ruffians eighty guineas to stab the king, and Sir George Wakeman had undertaken to poison his majesty for ten thousand pounds. When, however, he was brought face to face with these men, he was unable to recognise them, a fact he accounted for by stating he was exhausted by prolonged examination.

All England was scared by revelations so horrible; 'the business of life,' writes Macpherson, 'was interrupted by confusion, panic, clamour, and dreadful rumours.' In London, two thousand catholics were cast into prison; houses were daily searched for arms and treasonable documents; and in good time merciless executions filled up the sum of bitter persecutions.

One of the first victims of this so-called plot

was William Staley, a catholic banker of fair renown. The manner in which his life was sacrificed will serve as an example of the injustice meted to those accused. One day, William Staley happened to enter a pastrycook's shop in Covent Garden, opposite his bank, where there chanced to stand at the time a fellow named Carstairs; one of the infamous creatures who, envious of the honours and riches heaped on Oates and Bedlow, resolved to make new discoveries and enjoy like rewards. At this time he was, as Bishop Burnet states, 'looking about where he could find a lucky piece of villainy.' Unfortunately the banker came under his notice, and Bedlow and an associate pretended to have heard Staley say the king was a rogue and a persecutor of the people, whom he would stab if no other man was found to do the deed. These words Carstairs wrote down, and next morning called on the banker, showed him the treasonable sentence, and said he would swear it had been uttered by him, unless he, Staley, would purchase his silence. Though fully aware of his danger, he refused to do this; whereon Carstairs had him instantly arrested and committed for trial. Hearing of his situation, and knowing the infamous character of his accusers, Dr. Burnet thought it his duty to let the lord chancellor and the attorney-general know 'what profligate wretches these witnesses were.' His interference was received with hostility. The attorney-general took it ill that he should disparage the king's evidence; Lord Shaftesbury avowed those who sought to undermine the credit of witnesses were to be looked on as public enemies; whilst the Duke of Lauderdale said Burnet desired to save Staley because of the regard he had for anyone who would murder his majesty. Frightened by such remarks at a time when no man's life or credit was safe, Burnet shrank from further action; but rumour of his interference having got noised abroad, it was resented by the public to such an extent, that he was advised not to stir abroad for fear of public affronts.

Within five days of his arrest, William Staley was condemned to death. In vain he protested his innocence, pointed out the improbability of his using such words in a public room, and referred to his character as a loyal man and worthy citizen. He was condemned and executed as a traitor.

The next victim was Coleman. He denied having hired assassins to murder his majesty, or entertained desires for his death; but honestly stated he had striven to advance his religion, not by bloodshed, but by tolerance. Whilst lying in chains at Newgate prison under sentence of death, members of both Houses of Parliament visited him, and offered him pardon if he confessed a knowledge of the plot; but, in answer to all persuasions and promises, he avowed his innocence; protesting which, he died at Tyburn.

A little later, three Jesuits, named Ireland, Whitehead, and Fenwick, and two attendants of the queen's chapel, named Grove and Pickering, were executed on a charge of conspiracy to kill the king. Oates and Bedlow swore these Jesuits had promised Grove fifteen hundred pounds as price of the murder; Pickering chose as his reward to have thirty thousand masses, at a shilling a mass, said for him. Three times they had attempted this deed with a pistol; but once the flint was loose, another time there was no powder in the pan, and again the pistol was charged only with bullets. These five men died denying their guilt to the last.

Meanwhile, Dr. Tonge, the ingenious inventor of the plot, had sunk into insignificance by comparison with his audacious pupil. Not only did the latter have apartments at Whitehall allotted him, and receive a pension of twelve hundred a year, but he was lauded as the saviour of his country, complimented with the title of doctor of divinity, honoured in public and entertained in private. Eachard mentions 'a great supper in the city,' given in compliment to Oates by 'twenty eminent rich citizens;' and Sir John Reresby writes of meeting him at the dinner-table of Dr. Gunning, Bishop of Ely. Nothing could exceed the insolence and arrogance of the impostor. He appeared in a silk gown and cassock, a long scarf, a broad hat with satin band and rose, and called himself a doctor of divinity. No man dared contradict or oppose him, lest he should be denounced as a conniver of the plot, and arrested as a traitor. 'Whoever he pointed at was taken up and committed,' says North. 'So that many people got out of his way as from a blast, and glad they could prove their last two years' conversation. The very breath of him was pestilential, and if it brought not imprisonment, it surely poisoned reputation.' Sir John, speaking of him at the bishop's dinner-table, says 'he was blown up with the hopes of running down the Duke of York, and spoke of him and his family after a manner which showed himself both a fool and a knave. He reflected not only on him personally, but upon her majesty; nobody daring to contradict him, for fear of being made a party to the plot. I at least did not undertake to do it, when he left the room in some heat. The bishop told me this was his usual discourse, and that he had checked him formerly for taking so indecent a liberty, but he found it was to no purpose.'

The impostor's conversation on this occasion furnishes the key-note of a vile plot now contrived to intercept the lawful succession, either by effectually removing the queen, and thereby enabling the king to marry again; or otherwise excluding the Duke of York by act of parliament from lawful right to the crown. Though Shaftesbury's hand was not plainly seen, there can be no doubt it was busily employed in working out his favourite design.

The blow was first aimed at her majesty by Bedlow, who, on the 25th of November, accused her of conspiring to kill her husband. About eighteen months previously, he said, there had been a consultation in the chapel gallery at Somerset House, which had been attended by Lord Bellasis, Mr. Coleman, La Faire, Pritchard, Latham, and Sheldon, four Jesuits, and two Frenchmen whom he took to be abbots, two persons of quality whose faces he did not see, and lastly by her majesty. The Jesuits afterwards confided in him as a person of trust, that the queen wept at a proposal to murder the king which had been made, but subsequently yielding to arguments of the French abbots, had consented to the design. Indeed, Bedlow, who was in the sacristy when her majesty passed through at the termination of this meeting, noticed her face had much changed. Here his story ended; but, as was now usual, it was taken up and concluded by Oates.

Appearing at the Bar of the House of Commons, this vile impostor cried out, 'Aye, Taitus

Oates, accause Caatharine, Quean of England, of haigh traison.' Then followed his audacious evidence. In the previous July, Sir George Wakeham, in writing to a Jesuit named Ashby, stated her majesty would aid in poisoning the king. A few days afterwards, Harcourt and four other Jesuits having been sent for, attended the queen at Somerset House. On that occasion Oates waited on them; they went into a chamber, he stayed without. Whilst there he heard a woman's voice say she would endure her wrongs no longer, but should assist Sir George Wakeham in poisoning the king. He was afterwards admitted to the chamber, and saw no woman there but her majesty; and he heard the same voice ask Harcourt, whilst he was within, if he had received the last ten thousand pounds.

The appetite of public credulity seeming to increase by that on which it fed, this avowal was readily believed. That the accusation had not been previously made; that Oates had months before sworn he knew no others implicated in the plot beyond those he named; that the queen had never interfered in religious matters; that she loved her husband exceeding well, were facts completely overlooked in the general agitation. Parliament 'was in a rage and flame;' and next day the Commons drew up an address to the king, stating that 'having received information of a most desperate and traitorous design against the life of his sacred majesty, wherein the queen is particularly charged and accused,' they besought him that 'she and all her family, and all papists and reputed papists, be forthwith removed from his court.' Furthermore, the House sent a message to the Peers, desiring their concurrence in this request; but the Lords made answer, before doing so they would examine the witnesses against her majesty. This resolution was loudly and indecently protested against by Lord Shaftesbury and two of his friends.

The king had discredited the story of the plot from the first; but remembering the unhappy consequences which had resulted upon the disagreement of the monarch and his parliament in the previous reign, he weakly resolved to let himself be carried away by the storm, rather than offer it resistance. On the condemnation of the Jesuits, he had appeared unhappy and dissatisfied; 'but,' says Lord Romney, 'after he had had a little advice he kept his displeasure to himself.' The Duke of York states, in the Stuart Papers, that 'the seeming necessity of his affairs made his majesty think he could not be safe but by consenting every day to the execution of those he knew in his heart to be most innocent.' Now, however, when foul charges were made against the queen, calculated not merely to ruin her honour but destroy her life, he resolved to interfere. He therefore requested she would return to Whitehall, where she should be safe under his protection; and feeling assured Oates had received instructions from others more villainous than their tool, he ordered a strict guard to be kept upon him. This he was, however, obliged to remove next day at request of the Commons.

On the examination before the House of Lords of Oates and Bedlow, their evidence proved so vague and contradictory that it was rejected even by the most credulous. When Bedlow was asked 'why he had not disclosed such a perilous matter in conjunction with his previous information touching the murder of Sir Edmondbury Godfrey,' he coolly replied, 'it had escaped his memory.' On Oates being sent to point out the apartment in which he had seen her majesty and the Jesuits, he first selected the guard-room, and afterwards the privy chamber, places in which it would have been impossible to have held secret consultation. Aware that the king was resolved to protect her majesty, and conscious the evidence of her accusers was more wildly improbable than usual, the Lords refused to second the address of the Commons, when the charge against this hapless woman was abandoned, to the great vexation of my Lord Shaftesbury.

· Though the queen happily escaped the toils of her enemies, the reign of terror was by no means at an end. At request of the king, the Duke of York left England and took refuge in Brussels; the catholic peers imprisoned in the Tower were impeached with high treason; Hill, Green and Berry, servants of her majesty, charged with the murder of Sir Edmondbury Godfrey, were, without a shadow of evidence, hurried to the scaffold, as were soon after Whitebread, Fenwick, Harcourt, Gavan and Turner, Jesuits all, and Langhorn, a catholic lawyer, for conspiring to murder the king. On the morning when these unfortunate men stood ignominiously bound to the gallows at Tyburn, the instruments of death before their eyes, the angry murmurs of the surging mob ringing in their ears, suddenly the sound of a voice crying aloud, 'A pardon! a pardon!' was heard afar off, and presently a horseman appeared riding at full speed. The soldiers with some difficulty making way for him through a line of excited people, he advanced to the foot of the scaffold, and handed a roll of paper bearing the king's seal to the sheriff, who, opening it, read a promise of pardon to those now standing face to face with death, provided 'they should acknowledge the conspiracy, and lay open what they knew thereof.' To this they replied they knew of no plot, and had never desired harm to the king; and, praying for those who had sought their lives, they died.

The firmness and patience with which the victims of judicial murder had one and all met death, refusing bribes, and resisting persuasions to own themselves guilty, could not fail in producing some effect upon the public mind; and towards the middle of the year 1679 the first signs of a reaction became visible, when three

Benedictine monks and the queen's physician were tried for conspiracy 'to poison the king, subvert the government, and introduce popery.' During the examination, Evelyn tells us, 'the bench was crowded with the judges, lord mayor, justices, and innumerable spectators.' After a tedious trial of nine hours, the jury brought the prisoners in not guilty, 'without,' says Evelyn, 'sufficient disadvantage and reflection on witnesses, especially on Oates and Bedlow.'

As my Lord Shaftesbury had not yet succeeded in his desired project of excluding the Duke of York from succession, the symptoms of change in public opinion were thoroughly distasteful to him. He therefore resolved to check them immediately, and stimulate the agitation and fear that had for many months reigned paramount throughout the nation. For this purpose he had recourse to his former method of circulating wild and baseless reports. Accordingly a rumour was soon brought before the House of Commons of a horrible plot hatched by the papists to burn London to the ground. This, it was alleged, would be effected by a servant-maid setting a clothes-press on fire in the house of her master, situated in Fetter Lane. Two vile Irishmen were to feed the flames, and meanwhile the catholics would rise in rebellion, and, assisted by an army of sixty thousand French soldiers, kill the king, and put all protestants to the sword. Though this tale was in due time discredited, yet it served its purpose in the present. The violent alarm it caused had not subsided when another terrible story, started on the excellent authority of Lord Shaftesbury's cook, added a new terror. This stated the Duke of York had placed himself at the head of the French troops, with intention of landing in England, murdering the king, and forcing papacy on his subjects. The scare was sufficiently effectual to cause parliament to petition his majesty that he might revoke all licenses recently granted catholic householders to reside in the capital; and order the execution of all priests who administered sacraments or celebrated mass within the kingdom. Soon after this address, Lord Russell was sent by the Commons to the Peers, requesting their concurrence in the statement that 'the Duke of York's being a papist, the hope of his coming to the crown had given the greatest countenance and encouragement to the conspiracies and designs of the papists.' And now, in May, 1679, the condition of popular feeling promising well for its success, the Bill of Exclusion was introduced, ordaining that 'James Duke of York should be incapable of inheriting the crowns of England and Ireland; that on the demise of his majesty without heirs of his body, his dominions should devolve, as if the Duke of York were also dead, on that person next in succession who had always professed the protestant religion established by law.' This passed the House of Commons by a majority of seventy-nine votes.

Alarmed by this bill, Charles resolved to show signs of resentment, and at the same time check the increasing power of the commons, by a sudden and decisive movement. Therefore, without previously hinting at his intentions, he prorogued parliament before the bill was sent to the House of Lords. This was a keen surprise to all, and a bitter disappointment to Shaftesbury, who vowed those who advised the king to this measure should answer for it with their heads. Owing to various delays, the Bill of Exclusion was not brought before the Peers until eighteen months later. Its introduction was followed by a debate lasting six hours, in which Shaftesbury distinguished himself by his force and bitterness. At nine o'clock at night the House divided, when the measure was rejected by a majority of thirty-three votes, amongst which were those of the fourteen bishops present.

Mortified by this unexpected decision, the violent passions of the defeated party hurried them on to seek the blood of those peers lodged in the Tower. Of the five, William Howard, Viscount Stafford—youngest son of the Earl of Arran, and nephew of the Duke of Norfolk—was selected to be first put upon his trial; inasmuch as, being over sixty years, and a sufferer from many infirmities, it was judged he would be the least capable of making a vigorous defence. Three perjured witnesses swore he had plotted against the king's life, but no proof was forthcoming to support their evidence. Notwithstanding this was 'bespattered and falsified in almost every point,' it was received as authentic by the judges, who made a national cause of his prosecution, and considered no punishment too severe for a papist. After a trial of five days sentence of death was pronounced upon him, and on the 29th of December, 1680, he was beheaded on Tower Hill.

Like those who had suffered from similar charges, he protested his innocence to the last; but his words met with a reception different from theirs. Their dying speeches had been greeted by groans, hisses, and signs of insatiable fury; but his declarations fell upon silent and sympathizing hearts. When he had made denial of the crimes of which he was accused, a great cry rose from the mob, 'We believe you —we believe you, my lord;' and then a single voice calling out 'God bless you!' the words were taken up and repeated by a vast throng, so that the last sounds he heard on earth were those of prayer. He died with a firmness worthy of his caste. Having laid his head upon the block, the executioner brandished his axe in the air, and then set it quietly down at his feet. Raising his head, Lord Stafford inquired the cause of delay; the executioner replied he awaited a sign. 'Take your time,' said he who stood at the verge of eternity; 'I shall make no sign.' He who held the axe in his hand hesitated a second, and then said in a low and troubled voice, 'Do you forgive me, sir?' To which Lord Stafford made brief answer, 'I do.' Then he laid his head again upon the blood-stained block. Once more the glitter of steel flashed through the air, a groan arose from the crowd, and Lord Stafford's head was severed from his body.

A reaction now set in, and gained strength daily. The remaining peers were in due time liberated; the blood of innocent victims was no longer shed; and the Duke of York was recalled. Such was the end of the popish plot, which, says Archdeacon Eachard, 'after the strictest and coolest examinations, and after a full length of time, the government could find very little foundation to support so vast a fabrick, besides downright swearing and assurance; not a gun, sword, nor dagger, not a flask of powder or dark lanthorn, to effect this strange villainy, and with the exception of Coleman's writings, not one slip of an original letter of commission among those great numbers alledged to uphold the reputation of the discoveries.'

Concerning those through whose malice such disturbance was wrought, and so much blood shed, a few words may be added. Within twelve months of Lord Stafford's execution, Shaftesbury was charged with high treason, but escaping condemnation, fled from further molestation to Holland, where, after a residence of six weeks, he died. Tonge departed this life in 1680, unbenefited by the monstrous plot he had so skilfully devised; and in the same year Bedlow was carried to the grave after an illness of four days. Oates survived to meet a share of the ignominy and punishment due to his crimes. After a residence of three years in Whitehall, he was driven out of the palace on account of 'certain misdemeanors laid to his charge,' and deprived of his salary. Two years later, in May, 1683, he was accused of calling the Duke of York a traitor, and using scandalous words towards his royal highness. Upon hearing of the case the jury fined him one hundred thousand pounds. Unable to pay the sum, he was cast into prison, where he remained six years, until liberated in the reign of William and Mary. His punishment was not, however, at an end. At the Michaelmas term of 1684 he was accused of having wilfully perjured himself at the late trials. As he pleaded not guilty, his case was appointed to be heard at the King's Bench Court. His trial did not take place until May, 1685, on which occasion the lord chief justice, in summing up the evidence, declared, 'There does not remain the slightest doubt that Oates is the blackest and most perjured villain on the face of the earth.'

After a quarter of an hour's absence from court, the jury returned a verdict of guilty, and sentence was pronounced against him. He was stripped of his canonical habit; forced to walk through all the courts of Westminster Hall proclaiming his crimes; to stand an hour on the pillory opposite Westminster Hall gate on Monday; an hour on the pillory at the Royal Exchange on Tuesday; and on Wednesday he was tied to a cart and whipt at the hands of the common hangman from Aldgate to Newgate, in the presence, says Eachard, 'of innumerable spectators, who had a more than ordinary curiosity to see the sight.'

CHAPTER VIII.

London under Charles II.—Condition and appearance of the thoroughfares.—Coffee is first drunk in the capital.—Taverns and their frequenters.—The city by night.—Wicked people do creep about.—Companies of young gentlemen.—The Duke of Monmouth kills a beadle.—Sir Charles Sedley's frolic.—Stately houses of the nobility.—St. James's Park.—Amusement of the town.—At Bartholomew Fair.—Bull, bear, and dog fights.—Some quaint sports.

DURING the first six years of the merry monarch's reign, London town, east of Temple Bar, consisted of narrow and tortuous streets of quaintly gabled houses, pitched roofed and plaster fronted. Scarce four years had passed after the devastating fire which laid this portion of the capital in ashes, when a new and stately city rose upon the ruins of the old. Thoroughfares lying close by the Thames, which were wont to suffer from inundations, were raised;

DUCHESS OF MAZARINE.

those which from limited breadth had caused inconvenience and bred pestilence were made wide; warehouses and dwellings of solid brick and carved stone, with doors, window-frames, and breastsummers of stout oak, replaced irregular though not unpicturesque habitations; whilst the halls of companies, eminent taverns, and abodes of great merchants, were now built 'with fair courtyards before them, and pleasant gardens behind them, and fair spacious rooms and galleries in them, little inferior to some princes' palaces.' Moreover, churches designed by the genius of Christopher Wren, adorned with spires, steeples, and minarets, intersected the capital at all points.

This new, handsome, and populous city presented an animated, ever changing, and merry scene. From 'the high street which is called the Strand,' far eastwards, great painted signs, emblazoned with heraldic arms, or ornamented with pictures of grotesque birds and animals, swung above shop-doors and taverns. Stalls laden with wares of every description, 'set out with decorations as valuable as those of the stage,' extended into the thoroughfares. In the new

Exchange, built by the worshipful company of mercers at a cost of eight thousand pounds, and adorned by a fair statue of King Charles II. in the habit of a Roman emperor, were galleries containing rows of very rich shops, displaying manufactures and ornaments of rare description, served by young men known as apprentices, and likewise by comely wenches.

At corners and nooks of streets, under eaves of churches and great buildings, and other places of shelter, sat followers of various trades and vendors of divers commodities, each in the place which had become his from daily association and long habit. These good people, together with keepers of stalls and shops, extolled their wares in deafening shouts; snatches of song, shouts of laughter, and the clang of pewter vessels came in bursts of discord from open tavern doors; women discoursed with or abused each other, according to their temper and inclination as they leaned from the jutting small-paned windows and open balconies of their homesteads; hackney coaches or 'hell carts,' as they drove by, cast filth and refuse lying in kennels upon the clothes of passengers; the carriers of sedan-chairs deposited their burthens to fight for right of way in narrow passages and round crowded corners.

Through the busy concourse flowing up and down the thoroughfares from dawn to dusk, street-criers took their way, bearing wares upon their heads in wicker baskets, before them on broad trays, or slung upon their backs in goodly packs. And as they passed, their voices rose above the general din, calling 'Fair lemons and oranges, oranges and citrons!' 'Cherries, sweet cherries, ripe and red!' 'New flounders and great plaice; buy my dish of great eels!' 'Rosemary and sweet briar; who'll buy my lavender?' 'Fresh cheese and cream!' 'Lily-white vinegar!' 'Dainty sausages!' which calls, being frequently intoned to staves of melody, fell with pleasant sounds upon the ear.* Moreover, to these divers sights and sounds were added ballad singers, who piped ditties upon topics of the day; quacks who sold nostrums and magic potions; dancers

* These hawkers so seriously interfered with legitimate traders, that in 1694 they were forbidden to sell any goods or merchandise in any public place within the city or liberties, except in open markets and fairs, on penalty of forty shillings for each offence, both to buyers and sellers.

who performed on tight-ropes; wandering musicians; fire-eaters of great renown; exhibitors of dancing dolls, and such like itinerants 'as make show of motions and strange sights,' all of whom were obliged to have and to hold ' a license in red and black letters, under the hand and seal of Thomas Killigrew, Esq., master of the revels to his sacred majesty Charles II.'

Adown the Strand, Fleet Street, and in that part of the city adjoining the Exchange, coffee-houses abounded in great numbers. Coffee, which in this reign became a favourite beverage, was introduced into London a couple of years before the restoration. It had, however, been brought into England at a much earlier period. John Evelyn, in the year 1638, speaks of it being drunk at Oxford, where there came to his college 'one Nathaniel Conoposis out of Greece, from Cyrill the patriarch of Constantinople, who, returning many years after, was made Bishop of Smyrna.' Twelve good years later, a coffee-house was opened at Oxford by one Jacobs, a Jew, where this beverage was imbibed 'by some who delighted in novelty.' It was, however, according to Oldys the antiquarian, untasted in the capital till a Turkey merchant named Edwards brought to London a Ragusan youth named Pasqua Rosee, who prepared this drink for him daily. The eagerness to taste the strange beverage drawing too much company to his board, Edwards allowed the lad, together with a servant of his son-in-law, to sell it publicly; whence coffee was first sold in St. Michael's Alley in Cornhill by Pasqua Rosee, 'at the sign of his own head,' about the year 1658.

Though coffee-drinkers first met with much ridicule from wits about town, and writers of broadsheet ballads, the beverage became gradually popular, and houses for its sale quickly multiplied. Famous amongst these, in the reign of the merry monarch, besides that already mentioned, was Garraway's in Exchange Alley; the Rainbow, by the Inner Temple Gate; Dick's, situated at No. 8, Fleet Street; Jacob's, the proprietor of which moved in 1671 from Oxford to Southampton Buildings, Holborn; the Grecian in the Strand, 'conducted without ostentation or noise;' the Westminster, noted as a resort of peers and members of parliament; and Will's, in Russell Street, frequented by the poet Dryden.

These houses, the forerunners of clubs, were, according to their situation and convenience, frequented by noblemen and men of quality, courtiers, foreign ministers, politicians, members of learned professions, wits, citizens of various grades, and all who loved to exchange greetings and gossip with their neighbours and friends. Within these low-ceilinged comfortable coffee-house rooms, fitted with strong benches and oak chairs, where the black beverage was drunk from handless wide brimmed cups, Pepys passed many cheerful hours, hearing much of the news he so happily narrates, and holding pleasant discourse with many notable men. It was in a coffee-house he encountered Major Waters, 'a deaf and most amorous melancholy gentleman, who is under a despayer in love, which makes him bad company, though a most good-natured man.' And in such a place he listened to 'some simple discourse about quakers being charmed by a string about their wrists;' and saw a certain merchant named Hill ' that is a master of most sorts of musique and other things, the universal character, art of memory, counterfeiting of hands, and other most excellent discourses.'

In days before newspapers came into universal circulation, and general meetings were known, coffee-houses became recognised centres for exchange of thought and advocacy of political action. Aware of this, the government, under leadership of Danby, not desiring to have its motives too freely canvassed, in 1675 issued an order that such 'places of resort for idle and disaffected persons' should be closed. Alarmed by this command, the keepers of such houses petitioned for its withdrawal, at the same time faithfully promising libels should not be read under their roofs. They were therefore permitted to carry on their business by license.

Next in point of interest to coffee-houses were taverns where men came to make merry, in an age when simplicity and goodfellowship largely obtained. As in coffee-houses, gossip was the order of the day in such places, each tavern being in itself 'a broacher of more news than hogsheads, and more jests than news.' Those of good standing and fair renown could boast rows of bright flagons ranged on shelves round panelled walls; of hosts, rotund in person and genial in manner; and of civil drawers, who could claim good breeding. The Bear, at the bridge-foot, situated at the Southwark side, was well known to men of gallantry and women of pleasure; and was, moreover, famous as the spot where the Duke of Richmond awaited Mistress Stuart on her escape from Whitehall. The Boar's Head, in Eastcheap, which gained pleasant mention in the plays of William Shakespeare, when rebuilt, after the great fire, became a famous resort. The Three Cranes, in the Vintry, was sacred to the shade of rare Ben Jonson. The White Bear's Head, in Abchurch Lane, where French dinners were served from five shillings a head 'to a guinea, or what sum you pleased,' was the resort of cavaliers. The Rose Tavern, in the Poultry, was famous for its excellent ale, and no less for its mighty pretty hostess, to whom the king had kissed hands as he rode by on his entry. The Rummer was likewise of some note, inasmuch as it was kept by one Samuel Prior, uncle to Matthew Prior, the ingenious poet. On the balcony of the Cock, near Covent Garden, Sir Charles Sedley had stood naked in a drunken frolic; and at the King's Head, over against the Inner

Temple Gate, Shaftesbury and his friends laid their plots, coming out afterwards on the double balcony in front, as North describes them, 'with hats and no peruques, pipes in their mouths, merry faces and dilated throats, for vocal encouragement of the canaglia below.'

All day long the streets were crowded by those whom business or diversion carried abroad; but when night fell apace, the keepers of stalls and shops speedily secured their wares and fastened their doors, whilst the honest citizen and his family kept within house. For the streets being unlighted, darkness fell upon them, relieved only as some person of wealth rode homewards from visiting a friend, or a band of late revellers returned from a feast, when the glare of flambeaux, carried by their attendants, for a moment brought the outlines of houses into relief, or flashed red light upon their diamond panes, leaving all in profound gloom on disappearing.

The condition of the thoroughfares favouring the inclination of many loose persons, they wandered at large, dealing mischief to those whose duty took them abroad. From the year 1556, in the reign of Queen Mary, 'fit persons with suitable strength' had been appointed to walk the streets and watch the city by night; to protect those in danger, arrest suspected persons, warn householders of danger by fire and candle, help the poor, pray for the dead, and preserve the peace. These burly individuals were known as watch or bell men; one was appointed for each ward, whose duty it was to pass through the district he guarded ringing his bell, 'and when that ceaseth,' says Stow, 'he salutes his masters and mistresses with his rhymes, suitable to the seasons and festivals of the year, and bids them look to their lights.'

In the third year of the reign of King Charles II., whilst Sir John Robinson was mayor of London town, divers good orders were made by him and his common council for the better service of these watches. The principal of these set forth that each should be accompanied by a constable and a beadle selected from the inhabitants of their respective wards, who should be required in turn to render voluntary service in guarding the city, from nine of the clock at night till seven in the morning, from Michaelmas to the

1st of April; and from that date until the 31st of March, from ten at night till five in the morning.

These rules were not, however, vigorously carried out; the volunteers were frequently unwilling to do duty, or when, fearful of fine, they went abroad, they usually spent their time in tippling in ale-houses, so that, as Delaune remarks, 'a great many wicked persons capable of the blackest villainies do creep about, as daily and sad experience shows.' It was not only those who, with drawn swords, darted from some deep porch or sheltering buttress, in hopes of enriching themselves at their neighbour's expense, that were to be dreaded. It was a fashion of the time for companies of young gentlemen to saunter forth in numbers after route or supper, when, being merry with wine and eager for adventure, they were brave enough to waylay the honest citizen and abduct his wife, beat the watch and smash his lantern, bedaub signboards and wrench knockers, overturn a sedan-chair and vanquish the carriers, sing roystering songs under the casements of peaceful sleepers, and play strange pranks to which they were prompted by young blood and high spirits.

Among those who made prominent figures in such unholy sports was the king's eldest son, my Lord Duke of Monmouth. He, and his young grace of Albemarle—son to that gallant soldier now deceased, who was instrumental in restoring his majesty—together with some seven or eight young gentlemen, whilst on their rounds one Sunday morning encountered a beadle, whose quaint and ponderous figure presented itself to their blithe minds as a fit object for diversion in lieu of better. Accordingly they accosted him with rough words and unceremonious usage, the which he resenting, they came to boisterous threats and many blows, that ended only when the poor fellow lay with outstretched limbs stark dead upon the pavement. Sir Charles Sedley and Lord Brockhurst were also notable as having been engaged in another piece of what has been called 'frolick and debauchery,' when 'they ran up and down all night almost naked through the streets, at last fighting and being beaten by the watch, and clapped up all night.'

It was not until the last years of the merry

monarch's reign that there was introduced 'an ingenious and useful invention for the good of this great city, calculated to secure one's goods, estates, and person; to prevent fires, robberies and housebreakings, and several accidents and casualties by falls to which man is liable by walking in the dark.' This was a scheme for lighting the streets, by placing an oil-lamp in front of every tenth house on each side of the way, from Michaelmas to Lady-day, every night from six of the clock till twelve, beginning the third night after every full moon, and ending on the sixth night after every new moon; one hundred and twenty nights in all. The originator of this plan was one Edward Hemming, of London, gentleman. His project was at first ridiculed and opposed by 'narrow-souled and self-interested people,' who were no doubt children of darkness and doers of evil deeds; but was eventually hailed with delight by all honest men, one of whom, gifted with considerable imagination, declared these poor oil-lamps 'seemed but one great solar light that turned nocturnal shades to noonday.'

In this reign the city proper was confined

eastward of Temple Bar; to the west lay the palaces of Somerset House and Whitehall, the stately parks, and great houses of the nobility surrounded by wide gardens and wooded grounds. Monsieur Sorbiere, who in this reign made a journey into England, an account of which he subsequently published 'to divert a person of quality who loved him extremely,' resided close by Covent Garden during his stay. It was usual, he writes, for people in the district to say, ' I go to London,' for 'indeed 'tis a journey for those who live near Westminster. 'Tis true,' he adds, ' they may sometimes get thither in a quarter of an hour by water, which they cannot do in less than two hours by land, for I am persuaded no less time will be necessary to go from one end of its suburb to the other.' For a crown a week this ingenious and travelled gentleman had lodgings in Covent Garden, not far removed from Salisbury House, a vicinity which he avows was 'certainly the finest place in the suburbs.' Covent Garden itself has been described by John Strype, native of the city of London, as ' a curious large and airy square enclosed by rails, between which railes and houses runs a fair street.' The square, or, as it was commonly called, garden, was well gravelled for greater accommodation of those who wished to take the air; and that its surface might more quickly dry after rain, it was raised by an easy ascent to the centre, where stood a sundial fixed on a black marble pillar, at the base of which were stone steps, 'whereon the weary might rest.'

The west side of the square was flanked by the handsome portico of St. Paul's Church, erected at the expense of Francis, Earl of Bedford, from designs by Mr. Inigo Jones; the south side opened to Bedford Gardens, 'where there is a small grotto of trees, most pleasant in the summer season.' Here, on Tuesdays, Thursdays, and Saturdays, a market was held, well stocked with roots, fruits, herbs, and flowers. On the north and east sides stood large and stately houses of persons of quality and consideration, the fronts of which, being supported by strong pillars, afforded broad walks, known as the Piazza, and found convenient in wet and sultry weather.

Here amongst other houses was that of my Lord Brouncker, where Mr. Pepys enjoyed a most noble French dinner and much good discourse, in return for which he gave much satisfaction by the singing of a new ballad, to wit, Lord Dorset's famous song, 'To all ye ladies now on land.' Not far distant, its face turned to the Strand, was the stately residence of the Duke of Bedford, a large dark building, fronted by a great courtyard, and backed by spacious gardens enclosed by red-brick walls. Likewise in the Strand stood Arundel House, the residence of Henry Frederick Howard, Earl of Arundel and Surrey, and Earl Marshal of England; Hatfield House, built by Thomas Hatfield, Bishop of Durham, as a town residence for himself and his heirs lawfully begotten; York House, richly adorned with the arms of Villiers and Manners—one gloomy chamber of which was shown as that wherein its late noble owner, George, first Duke of Buckingham, was stabbed by Felton; Worcester House, at one time occupied by Lord Chancellor Clarendon; and Essex House, situated near St. Clement Danes, the town residence of Arthur Capel, Earl of Essex, 'a sober, wise, judicious, and pondering person, not illiterate beyond the rate of most noblemen of this age.'

There were also many noble mansions lying westward, amongst them being those of the Dukes of Ormond and Norfolk in St. James's Square, which was built at this time; Berkeley House, which stood on the site now occupied by Berkeley Square, a magnificent structure containing a staircase of cedar wood, and great suites of lofty rooms; Leicester House, situated in Leicester Fields, subsequently known as Leicester Square, behind which stretched a goodly common; Goring House, 'a very pretty villa furnished with silver jars, vases, cabinets, and other rich furniture, even to wantonnesse and profusion,' on the site of which Arlington Street now stands; Clarendon House, a princely residence, combining 'state, use, solidity, and beauty,' surrounded by fair gardens, that presently gave place to Bond Street; Southampton House, standing, as Evelyn says, in 'a noble piazza—a little town,' now known as Bloomsbury Square, whose pleasant grounds commanded a full view of the rising hills of Hampstead and Highgate; and Montagu House, described as a palace built in the French fashion, standing on the ground now occupied by the

British Museum, which in this reign was backed by lonely fields, the dread scenes of 'robbery, murder, and every species of depravity and wickedness of which the heart can think.'

Besides the grounds and gardens surrounding these stately mansions, a further aspect of space and freshness, was added to the capital by public parks. Foremost amongst these was St. James's, to which the merry monarch added several fields, and for its greater advantage employed Monsieur La Notre, the famous French landscape-gardener. Amongst the improvements this ingenious man effected were planting trees of stately height, contriving a canal one hundred feet broad and two hundred and eighty feet long, with a decoy and duck island,* and making a pleasant pathway bordered by an aviary on either side, usually called Bird Cage Walk. An enclosure for deer was formed in the centre of the park; not far removed was the famous Physic Garden, where oranges were first seen in England; and

* The goodnatured Charles made Monsieur St. Evremond governor of Duck Island, to which position he attached a salary much appreciated by the exile. The island was removed in 1790 to make room for fresh improvements.

at the western end, where Buckingham Palace has been erected, stood Arlington House, described as 'a most neat box, and sweetly seated amongst gardens, enjoying the prospect of the park and the adjoining fields.'

The great attraction of St. James's Park was the Mall, which Monsieur Sorbier tells us was a walk 'eight hundred and fifty paces in length, beset with rows of large trees, and near a small wood, from whence you may see a fine mead, a long canal, Westminster Abbey, and the suburbs, which afford an admirable prospect.' This path was skirted by a wooded border, and at the extreme end was set with iron hoops, 'for the purpose of playing a game with a ball, called the mall.'*

In St. James's Park Samuel Pepys first saw the Duke of York playing at 'pelemele'; and

* Our Pall Mall is, I believe, derived from paille maille, a game somewhat analogous to cricket, and imported from France in the reign of the second Charles. It was formerly played in St. James's Park, and in the exercise of the sport a small hammer or mallet was used to strike the ball. I think it worth noting that the Malhe crest is a mailed arm and hand, the latter grasping a mallet.'—*Notes and Queries*, 1st series, vol. iii., p. 351.

likewise in 1662 witnessed with astonishment people skate upon the ice there, skates having been just introduced from Holland; on another occasion he enjoyed the spectacle of Lords Castlehaven and Arran running down and killing a stout buck for a wager before the king. And one sultry July day, meeting an acquaintance here, the merry soul took him to the farther end, where, seating himself under a tree in a corner, he sung him some blithesome songs. It was likewise in St. James's Park the Duke of York, meeting John Milton one day, asked him if his blindness was not to be regarded as a just punishment from heaven, due to his having written against the martyred king. 'If so, sir,' replied the great poet and staunch republican, 'what must we think of his majesty's execution upon a scaffold?' To which question his royal highness vouchsafed no reply.

It was a favourite custom of his majesty, who invariably rose betimes, to saunter in the park whilst the day was young, and pass an hour or two in stroking the heads of his feathered favourites in the aviary, feeding the fowls in the pond with biscuits, and playing with the crowd of spaniels ever attending his walks. For his greater amusement he had brought together in the park a rare and valuable collection of birds and beasts; amongst which were, according to a quaint authority, 'an onocratylus, or pelican, a fowl between a stork and a swan—a melancholy water-fowl brought from Astracan by the Russian ambassador.' This writer tells us, 'It was diverting to see how the pelican would toss up and turn a flat fish, plaice or flounder, to get it right into its gullet at its lower beak, which being filmy stretches to a prodigious wideness when it devours a great fish. Here was also a small water-fowl, not bigger than a more-hen, that went almost quite erect like the penguin of America. It would eate as much fish as its whole body weighed, yet ye body did not appear to swell the bigger. The Solan geese here are also great devourers, and are said soon to exhaust all ye fish in a pond. Here was a curious sort of poultry not much exceeding the size of a tame pidgeon, with legs so short as their crops seemed to touch ye earth; a milk-white raven; a stork which was a rarity at this season, seeing he was loose and could fly loftily;

two Balearian cranes, one of which having had one of his leggs broken, and cut off above the knee, had a wooden or boxen leg and thigh, with a joint so accurately made that ye creature could walke and use it as well as if it had ben natural; it was made by a souldier. The park was at this time stored with numerous flocks of severall sorts of ordinary and extraordinary wild fowle breeding about the decoy, which, looking neere so greate a citty, and among such a concourse of souldiers and people, is a singular and diverting thing. There are also deere of several countries, white, spotted like leopards; antelopes, an elk, red deere, roebucks, staggs, Guinea goates, Arabian sheepe, etc. There are withy-potts or nests for the wild fowle to lay their eggs in, a little above ye surface of ye water.'

Hyde Park, lying close by, likewise afforded a pleasant and convenient spot for recreation. Here, in a large circle railed off and known as the Ring, the world of quality and fashion took the air in coaches. The king and queen, surrounded by a goodly throng of maids of honour and gentlemen in waiting, were wont to ride here on summer evenings, whilst courtiers and citizens looked on the brilliant cavalcade with loyal delight. Horse and foot races were occasionally held in the park, as were reviews likewise. Cosmo, Grand Duke of Tuscany, 'a very jolly and good comely man,' whilst visiting England in 1669, was entertained by his majesty with a military parade held here one Sunday in May.

On arriving at Hyde Park, he found a great concourse of people and carriages waiting the coming of his majesty, who presently appeared with the Duke of York and many lords and gentlemen of the court. Having acknowledged an enthusiastic greeting, Charles retired under shade of some trees, in order to protect himself from the sun, and then gave orders for the troops to march past. 'The whole corps,' says the Grand Duke, 'consisted of two regiments of infantry, and one of cavalry, and of three companies of the body-guard, which was granted to the king by parliament since his return, and was formed of six hundred horsemen, each armed with carabines and pistols, all well mounted and dressed, which are uniform in everything but colour. When they had marched by, without firing either a volley or a salvo, his majesty dismounted from his horse, and entering his carriage, retired to Whitehall.'

Besides such diversions as were enjoyed in the parks, the people had various other sources of public amusement; amongst these puppet-shows, exhibitions of strength and agility, bear-baiting, cock-fighting, and dancing obtained. Until the restoration, puppet-shows had not been seen for years; for these droll dolls, being regarded as direct agents of Satan, were discountenanced by the puritans. With the coming of his majesty they returned in vast numbers, and were hailed with great delight by the people. One of these exhibitions which found special favour with the town, and speedily drew great audiences of gallants and ladies of quality, was situated within the rails of Covent Garden. And so perfect were the marionettes of this booth in the performance of divers sad tragedies and gay comedies, that they had the honour of receiving a royal command to play before their majesties at Whitehall. Amongst the most famous tumblers, or, as they were then styled, posture-makers, of this reign were Jacob Hall the friend of my Lady Castlemaine, and Joseph Clarke, beloved by the citizens. Though the latter was 'a well-made man and rather gross than thin,' we are told he 'exhibited in the most natural manner almost every species of deformity and dislocation; he could dislocate his vertebræ so as to render himself a shocking spectacle; he could also assume all the uncouth faces he had seen at a Quakers' meeting, at the theatre, or any public place. He was likewise the plague of all the tailors about town. He would send for one of them to take measure of him, but would so contrive it as to have a most immoderate rising in one of his shoulders; when his clothes were brought home and tried upon him, the deformity was removed into the other shoulder, upon which the tailor begged pardon for the mistake, and mended it as fast as he could; but on another trial found him as straight-shouldered a man as one would desire to see, but a little unfortunate in a hump back. In fact, this wandering tumour puzzled all the workmen about town, who found it impossible to accommodate so changeable a customer.'

Florian Marchand, 'the water-spouter,' was

another performer who enjoyed considerable fame. Such was the dexterity of this conjurer that, 'drinking only fountaine-water, he rendered out of his mouth in severall glasses all sorts of wine and sweete waters.' A Turk, who walked up an almost perpendicular line by means of his toes, danced blindfold on a tight rope with a boy dangling from his feet, and stood on his head on the top of a high mast, shared an equal popularity with Barbara Vanbeck, the bearded woman, and 'a monstrous beast, called a dromedary.' These wondrous sights, together with various others of a like kind, which were scattered throughout the town and suburbs during the greater part of the year, assembled in full strength at the fairs of St. Margaret, Southwark, and St. Bartholomew, in Smithfield. These gatherings, which usually lasted a fortnight, were looked forward to with considerable pleasure, and frequented not only by citizens bent on sport, but by courtiers in search of adventure.

Nay, even her majesty was tempted on one occasion to go a-fairing, as we gather from a letter addressed to Sir Robert Paston, contained in Ives's select papers. 'Last week,' says the writer thereof, 'the queen, the Duchess of Richmond, and the Duchess of Buckingham had a frolick to disguise themselves like country lasses, in red petticoats, waistcoats, etc., and so goe see the faire. Sir Bernard Gascoign, on a cart jade, rode before the queen; another stranger before the Duchess of Buckingham, and Mr. Roper before Richmond. They had all so overdone it in their disguise, and look'd so much more like antiques than country volk, that as soon as they came to the faire, the people began to goe after them; but the queen going to a booth to buy a pair of yellow stockins for her sweethart, and Sir Bernard asking for a pair of gloves, sticht with blew, for his sweethart, they were soon, by their gebrish, found to be strangers, which drew a bigger flock about them. One amongst them [who] had seen the queen at dinner, knew her, and was proud of her knowledge. This soon brought all the faire into a crowd to stare at the queen. Being thus discovered, they as soon as they could got to their horses; but as many of the faire as had horses, got up with their wives, children, sweetharts, or neighbours behind them, to get as much gape as they could till they brought them to the court gate. Thus by ill conduct was a merry frolick turned into a penance.'

On another occasion my Lady Castlemaine went to Bartholomew fair to see the puppets play 'Patient Grissel;' and there was the street 'full of people expecting her coming out,' who, when she appeared, 'suffered her with great respect to take the coach.' Not only the king's mistress, but likewise the whole court went to St. Margaret's fair to see 'an Italian wench daunce and performe all the tricks on the high rope to admiration; and monkies and apes do other feates of activity.' 'They,' says a quaint author, 'were gallantly clad *à la mode*, went upright, saluted the company, bowing and pulling off their hats, with as good a grace as if instructed by a dancing master. They turned heels over head with a basket having eggs in it, without breaking any; also with lighted candles on their heads, without extinguishing them; and with vessels of water, without spilling a drop.'

The cruel sport of bull and bear baiting was also commonly practised. Seated round an amphitheatre, the people witnessed these unfortunate animals being torn to pieces by dogs, the owners of which frequently jumped into the arena to urge them to their sanguinary work, on the result of which great wagers depended. Indignation arising against those who witnessed such sights may be somewhat appeased by the knowledge that infuriated bulls occasionally tossed the torn and bleeding carcases of their tormentors into the faces and laps of spectators. Pepys frequently speaks of dense crowds which assembled to witness this form of cruelty, which he designates as good sport; and Evelyn speaks of a gallant steed that, under the pretence that he had killed a man, was baited by dogs, but fought so hard for his life 'the fiercest of them could not fasten on him till he was run through with swords.' Not only bull and bear baiting, cock and dog fighting were encouraged, but prize combats between man and man were regarded as sources of great diversion. Pepys gives a vivid picture of a furious encounter he, in common with a great and excited crowd, witnessed at the bear-garden stairs, at Bankside, between a butcher and a waterman. 'The former,' says he, 'had the better all along, till by-and-by the latter dropped his sword out of his hand; and the butcher, whether not seeing his sword dropped I know not, but did give him a cut over the wrist, so as he was disabled to fight any longer. But Lord! to see how in a minute the whole stage was full of watermen to revenge the foul play, and the butchers to defend their fellow, though most blamed him; and then they all fell to it to knocking down and cutting many on each side. It was pleasant to see, but that I stood in the pit, and feared that in the tumult I might get some hurt.'

Among the more healthy sports which obtained during the reign were horse-racing, tennis, and bowling. The monarch had, at vast expense, built a house and stables at Newmarket, where he and his court regularly repaired, to witness racing. Here likewise the king and 'ye jolly blades enjoyed dauncing, feasting, and revelling, more resembling a luxurious and abandoned route than a Christian court.' He had likewise a tennis-court and bowling-green at Whitehall, where, at noonday and towards eve, blithe lords, and ladies in brave apparel, might be seen at play. Bowling was a game to which the people were much devoted, every suburban tavern having its green, where good friends and honest neighbours challenged each other's strength and skill. And amongst other pleasant sports and customs were those practised on May-day, when maids rose betimes to bathe their faces in dew, that they might become sweet-complexioned to men's sight; and milk-maids with garlands of spring flowers upon their pails, and posies in their breasts, danced to the merry music of fiddles adown the streets.

CHAPTER IX.

Court customs in the days of the merry monarch.—Dining in public.—The Duke of Tuscany's supper to the king.—Entertainment of guests by mountebanks.—Gaming at court.—Lady Castlemaine's losses.—A fatal duel.—Dress of the period.—Riding-habits first seen.—His majesty invents a national costume.—Introduction of the penny post.—Divorce suits are known.—Society of Antiquaries. Lord Worcester's inventions.—The Duchess of Newcastle.

FEW courts have been more brilliant than that of the merry monarch. All the beauty of fair women, the gallantry of brave men, and the gaiety of well-approved wits could compass, perpetually surrounded his majesty, making the royal palace a lordly pleasure-house. Noble banquets, magnificent balls, and brilliant suppers followed each other in quick succession. Three times a week—on Wednesdays, Fridays, and Sundays—the king and queen dined publicly in ancient state, whilst rare music was discoursed, and many ceremonies observed, amongst these being that each servitor of the royal table should eat some bread dipped in sauce of the dish he bore. On these occasions meats for the king's table were brought from the kitchen by yeomen of the guard, or beef-eaters. These men, selected as being amongst the handsomest, strongest, and tallest in England, were dressed in liveries of red cloth, faced with black velvet, having the king's cipher on the back, and on the breast the emblems of the Houses of York and Lancaster. By them the dishes were handed to the gentlemen in waiting, who served royalty upon their knees. 'You see,' said Charles one day to the Chevalier de Grammont, 'how I am waited on.' 'I thank your majesty for the explanation,' said the saucy Frenchman; 'I thought they were begging pardon for offering you so bad a dinner.'*

The costliness and splendour of some royal entertainments require the description of an eye-witness to be fully realized. Evelyn, speaking of a great feast given to the Knights of the

* This mode of serving the sovereign continued unto the coming of George I.

Garter in the banqueting-hall, tells us 'the king sat on an elevated throne, at the upper end of the table alone, the knights at a table on the right hand, reaching all the length of the roome; over against them a cupboard of rich gilded plate; at the lower end the musick; on the balusters above, wind musick, trumpets, and kettle-drums. The king was served by the lords and pensioners who brought up the dishes. About the middle of the dinner the knights drank the king's health, then the king theirs, when the trumpets and musick plaid and sounded, the guns going off at the Tower. At the banquet came in the queene and stood by the king's left hand, but did not sit. Then was the banquetting stuff flung about the roome profusely. In truth the crowd was so great that I now staied no longer than this sport began for fear of disorder. The cheere was extraordinary, each knight having forty dishes to his messe, piled up five or six high.'

Concerning the habit mentioned by Evelyn, of mobs rushing into banquet-halls, in order to possess themselves of all on which they could lay hands, many instances are mentioned. The Duke of Tuscany, amongst other authorities, narrates the inconvenience it caused at a supper he gave the king. When his majesty drove to the duke's residence he was preceded by trumpeters and torch-bearers, attended by the horse-guards and a retinue of courtiers, and accompanied by a vast crowd. On alighting from the coach the Duke of Tuscany, together with the noblemen and gentlemen of his household, received and conducted him through passages lighted by torches to the banquet-hall. From the ceiling of this saloon was suspended a chandelier of rock crystal, blazing with tapers; beneath it stood a circular table, at the upper end of which was placed a chair of state for the king. The whole entertainment was costly and magnificent. As many as eighty dishes were set upon the table; foreign wines, famous for great age and delicate flavour, sparkled in goblets of chased gold; and finally, a dessert of Italian fruits and Portuguese sweetmeats was served. But scarce had this been laid upon the board, when the impatient crowd which had gathered round the house and forced its way inside to witness the banquet, now violently burst into the saloon and carried away all that lay before them. Neither the presence of the king nor the appearance of his soldiers guarding the entrance with carbines was sufficient to prevent entrance or hinder pillage. Charles, used to such scenes, left the table and retired into the duke's private apartments.

A quaint and curious account of a less ceremonious and more convivial feast, also graced by the king's presence, was narrated by Sir Hugh Cholmely to a friend and gossip. This supper was given by Sir George Carteret, a man of pleasant humour, and moreover treasurer of the navy. By the time the meats were removed, the king and his courtiers waxed exceedingly merry, when Sir William Armorer, equerry to his majesty, came to him and swore, '" By God, sir," says he, " you are not so kind to the Duke of York of late as you used to be." "Not I?" says the king. "Why so?" "Why," says he, "if you are, let us drink his health." "Why, let us," says the king. Then he fell on his knees and drank it; and having done, the king began to drink it. "Nay, sir," says Armorer; " by God, you must do it on your knees!" So he did, and then all the company; and having done it, all fell acrying for joy, being all maudlin and kissing one another, the king the Duke of York, the Duke of York the king; and in such a maudlin pickle as never people were.'

Throughout this reign the uttermost hospitality and good-fellowship abounded. Scarce a day passed that some noble house did not throw open its doors to a brilliant throng of guests; few nights grew to dawn that the vicinities of St. James's and Covent Garden were not made brilliant by the torches of those accompanying revellers to their homes. The fashionable hour for dinner was three of the clock, and for greater satisfaction of guests it now became the mode to entertain them after that meal with performances of mountebanks and musicians. Various diaries inform us of this custom. When my Lord Arlington* had bidden his friends to a

---

* At a great dinner given by this nobleman, Evelyn, who was present, tells us that Lord Stafford, the unfortunate nobleman afterwards executed on Tower Hill, 'rose from the table in some disorder, because there were roses stuck about the fruite when the descert was set on the table; such an antipathie it seems he had to them, as once Lady St. Leger also had, and to that degree, that, as Sirr Kenelm Digby tells us, laying but a rose upon her cheeke when she was asleepe, it raised a blister; but Sir Kenelm was a teller of strange things.'

feast, he subsequently diverted them by the tricks of a fellow who swallowed a knife in a horn sheath, together with several pebbles, which he made rattle in his stomach, and produced again, to the wonder and amusement of all who beheld him. The master of the mint, worthy Mr. Slingsby, a man of finer taste, delighted his guests with the performances of renowned good masters of music, one of whom, a German, played to great perfection on an instrument with five wire strings called the *viol d'amore;* whilst my Lord Sunderland treated his visitors to a sight of Richardson, the renowned fire eater, who was wont to devour brimstone on glowing coals; melt a beer-glass and eat it up; take a live coal on his tongue, on which he put a raw oyster, and let it remain there till it gaped and was quite broiled; take wax, pitch and sulphur, and drink them down flaming; hold a fiery hot iron between his teeth, and throw it about like a stone from hand to hand, and perform various other prodigious feats.

Other means of indoor amusement were practised in those days, which seem wholly incompatible with the gravity of the nation in these latter times. Pepys tells us that going to the court one day he found the Duke and Duchess of York, with all the great ladies, sitting upon a carpet on the ground playing 'I love my love with an A, because he is so-and-so; and I hate him with an A, because of this and that;' and some of the ladies were mighty witty, and all of them very merry. Grown persons likewise indulged in games of blind man's buff, and amusements of a like character; whilst at one time, the king, queen, and the whole court falling into much extravagance, as Burnet says, 'went about masked, and came into houses unknown, and danced there with a great deal of wild frolic. In all this they were so disguised, that without being in the secret, none could distinguish them. They were carried about in hackney chairs. Once the queen's chairmen, not knowing who she was, went from her; so she was alone and was much disturbed, and came to Whitehall in a hackney coach; some say it was in a cart.'

Dancing was also a favourite and common amusement amongst all classes. Scarce a week went by that Whitehall was not lighted up for a ball, at which the king, queen, and courtiers danced bransles, corants, and French figures;* and no night passed but such entertainments were likewise held in the city. Billiards and chess were also played, whilst gambling became a ruling passion. The queen, Duchess of York, and Duchess of Cleveland had each her card-table, around which courtiers thronged to win and lose prodigious sums. The latter being a thorough rake at heart, delighted in the excitement which hazard afforded; and the sums changing owners at her board were sometimes enormous. Occasionally she played for a thousand, or fifteen hundred pounds at a cast, and in a single night lost as much as twenty-five hundred guineas. It is related that once when playing basset she lost all her money; but, being unwilling to retire, and hopeful of regaining her losses, she asked young Churchill, on whom she had bestowed many favours, to lend her twenty pieces. Though the wily youth had a thousand

* The bransle, or brawl, had all the characteristics of a country-dance; several persons taking part in it, and all at various times joining hands. The corant was a swift lively dance, in which two persons only took part, and was not unlike our modern galop.

before him on the table, he coolly refused her request, on the plea that the bank—which he was then keeping—never lent. 'Not a person in the place,' says the narrator of this anecdote, 'but blamed him ; as to the duchess, her resentment burst out into a bleeding at her nose, and breaking of her lace, without which aid it is believed her vexation had killed her on the spot.'

The courtly Evelyn speaks of a certain Twelfthnight, when the king opened the revels in his privy chamber by throwing dice, and losing one hundred pounds; and Pepys describes the groomporters' rooms where gambling greatly obtained, and 'where persons of the best quality do sit down with people of any, though meaner.' Cursing and swearing, grumbling and rejoicing, were heard here to an accompanying rattle of guineas ; the whole causing dense confusion. And amongst the figures crouching round the tables of this hell, that of my Lord St. Albans was conspicuous. So great, indeed, was his passion for gambling, that when approaching his eightieth year, and quite blind, he was unable to renounce his love for cards, but with the help of a servant who named them to him, indulged himself in this way as of yore.

As may be expected, disputes, frequently ending in duels, continually arose betwixt those who gambled. Although the king had, on his restoration, issued a proclamation against this common practice, threatening such as engaged in it with displeasure, declaring them incapable of holding any office in his service, and forbidding them to appear at court, yet but little attention was paid his words, and duels continually took place. Though most frequently resorted to as a means of avenging outraged honour, they were occasionally the result of misunderstanding. A pathetic story is told of a fatal encounter, caused by a trifle light as air, which took place in the year 1667 at Covent Garden, between Sir Henry Bellasis and Tom Porter—the same witty soul who wrote a play called 'The Villain,' which was performed at the Duke's Theatre, and described as 'a pleasant tragedy.'

These worthy gentlemen and loyal friends loved each other exceedingly. One fatal day, both were bidden to dine with Sir Robert Carr, at whose table it was known all men drank freely; and having feasted, they two talked apart, when bluff Sir Henry, giving words of counsel to honest Tom, from force of earnestness spoke louder than his wont. Marvelling at this, some of those standing apart said to each other, 'Are they quarrelling, that they talk so high?' overhearing which the baronet replied in a merry tone, 'No, I would have you know I never quarrel but I strike; and take that as a rule of mine.' At these words Tom Porter, being anxious, after the manner of those who have drunk deep, to apprehend offence in speech of friend or foe, cried out he would like to see the man in England that durst give him a blow. Accepting this as a challenge, Sir Henry dealt him a stroke on the ear, which the other would have returned in anger but that they were speedily parted.

And presently Tom Porter, leaving the house full of resentment for the injury he had received, and of resolution to avenge it, met Mr. Dryden the poet, to whom he recounted the story. He concluded by requesting he might have his boy to bring him word which way Sir Henry Bellasis would drive, for fight he would that night, otherwise he felt sure they should be friends in the morning, and the blow would rest upon him. Dryden complying with his request, Tom Porter, still inflamed by fury, went to a neighbouring coffee-house, when presently word arrived Sir Harry's coach was coming that way. On this Tom Porter rushed out, stopped the horses, and bade the baronet alight. 'Why,' said the man, who but an hour before had been his best friend, 'you will not hurt me in coming out, will you?' 'No,' answered the other shortly. Sir Henry then descended, and both drew their swords. Tom Porter asked him if he were ready, and hearing he was, they fought desperately, till of a sudden a sharp cry was heard; Sir Henry's weapon fell upon the ground, and he placed one hand to his side, from which blood flowed freely. Then calling his opponent to him, he looked in his face reproachfully, kissed him lovingly, and bade him seek safety. 'For, Tom,' said he, struggling hard to speak, 'thou hast hurt me; but I will make shift to stand upon my legs till thou mayest withdraw, and the world not take notice of you, for,' continued he, with much tenderness, 'I would not have thee troubled for what thou hast done.' And the little crowd who had gathered around carried him to his coach; and twenty days later they followed him to his grave.

Throughout this merry reign, many fantastic changes took place in the costumes of courtiers and their followers. At the restoration, the dress most common to women of all ranks consisted of a gown with a laced stomacher and starched neckerchief, a sad-coloured cloak with a French hood, and a high-crowned hat. Such habiliments, admitting of little variety and less ornament, found no favour in the eyes of those who returned from foreign courts with the king, and therefore a change was gradually effected. The simple gown of wool and cotton gave place to loose and flowing draperies of silk and satin; the stiff neckerchief was removed to display fair shoulders and voluptuous breasts; the hat was bedecked by feathers of rare plumage and rich colour; the cloaks changed hues from sad to gay; the hoods being of 'yellow bird's eye,' and other bright tints. Indeed, the prodigal manner in which ladies of quality now exposed their bosoms, though pleasing to the court, became a matter of grave censure to worthy men. One of these in a pamphlet, entitled 'A Just and Seasonable Reprehension of Naked Breasts and Shoulders,' charges women of fashion with 'overlacing their gown bodies, and so thrusting up their breasts in order that they might show them half-naked.' It was not only at balls and in chambers of entertainment, he avowed, they appeared in this manner, but likewise at church, where their dress was 'not only immodest, but sometimes impudent and lascivious;' for they braved all dangers to have the satisfaction of being seen, and the consolation of giving pleasure.

The riding-habit, first introduced in 1664, caused considerable notice, and no small amount of mirth. The garb, as it was called, consisted of a doublet buttoned up the breast, a coat with long skirts, a periwig and tall hat, so that women clad in this fashion might be mistaken for men, if it were not for the petticoat which dragged under the coat. At the commencement of the reign, ladies of the court wore their hair after the French fashion, cut short in front and frizzed upon the forehead. When the queen arrived, her hair was arranged *à la négligence*, a mode declared mighty pretty; but presently a fashion came in vogue of wearing 'false locks set on wyres to make them stand at a distance from the head; as fardingales made the clothes stand out in Queen Elizabeth's reign.' Painting the face, which had been practised during the Commonwealth, became fashionable; as did likewise the use of patches and vizards or masks; which from the convenience they afforded wearers whilst witnessing an immoral play, or conducting a delicate intrigue, came greatly into use.

According to Randal Holmes's notes on dress, in the Harleian Library, the male costume at the restoration consisted of 'a short-waisted doublet, and petticoat breeches—the lining, being lower than the breeches, is tied above the knees. The breeches are ornamented with ribands up to the pocket, and half their breadth upon the thigh; the waistband is set about with ribands, and the shirt hanging out over them.' This dress gradually increased in richness and ornamentation: the doublet and breeches being changed from cloth to velvet and satin, the hat trimmed with plumes of gay feathers, and the neck adorned with bands of cambric, trimmed with Flanders and Brussels lace. The perfection and costliness to which the costume eventually reached is best shown by a description of Sir Richard Fanshaw, ambassador of the king, as presented in the diary of his spouse. 'Sir Richard was dressed,' she writes, 'in a very rich suit of clothes of a dark *fillemonte* brocade, laced with silver and gold lace—nine laces—every one as broad as my hand, and a little silver and gold lace laid between them, both of very curious workmanship; his suit was trimmed with scarlet taffety ribbon; his stockings of white silk upon long scarlet silk ones; his shoes black, with scarlet shoestrings and gaiters; his linen very fine, laced with rich Flanders lace; a black beaver buttoned on the left side with a jewel of twelve hundred pounds' value; a rich curious wrought gold chain, made in the Indies, at which hung the king his master's picture, richly set with diamonds; on his fingers he wore two rich rings; his gloves trimmed with the same ribbon as his clothes.'

The uttermost extravagance and luxury in dress now obtained; indeed, to such a passion and pride did it reach, that the monarch resolved on giving it some check by inventing a suit of plainer pretensions, which should become the national costume, and admit no change.

This determination he solemnly declared to his council in October, 1666, and on the 14th of the month appeared clad in a long vest slashed with white silk, reaching the knee, having the sword girt over it, a loose coat, straight Spanish breeches ruffled with black ribbons, and buskins instead of shoes and stockings. Though the habit was pronounced decent and becoming to his majesty, and was quickly adopted by the courtiers, there were those amongst his friends who offered him a wager he would not persist in wearing it long. At this the king stated his resolution afresh of never changing; but before the month was out he had made an alteration, for inasmuch as the vest, being slashed with white, was said by a wag to make the wearers look like magpies, his majesty changed the colour of the silk to black. This 'manly and comely habit' might have become permanently the fashion, if the King of France, by way of ridiculing the merry monarch, had not caused his footmen to be clad in like manner. Therefore, in less than two years, this mode gave place to others more fantastical. The vest was retained, but the shape and material were altered; the surcoat of cloth was discarded for velvet and rich plush, adorned with buckles of precious stones and chains of gold; the Spanish leather boots were laid aside for high-heeled shoes with rosettes and silver buckles. Towards the close of the reign the costume became much plainer. Through all these varying fashions the periwig, introduced in 1663, held its own, increasing in length and luxuriance with time. On its first coming into general use, the clergy had cried out against it as ministering to the vanity and extravagance of the age; but in a while many of them adopted its use, for, as Granger remarks, 'it was observed that a periwig procured many persons a respect and even veneration which they were strangers to before, and to which they had not the least claim from their personal merit.'

Amongst other strange innovations and various

improvements known in this reign, the introduction of a penny post may be considered the most useful. King James I., of happy memory, had, in imitation of like regulations in other countries, established a general post for foreign parts; King Charles I. had given orders to Thomas Witherings, Esquire, his postmaster-general to settle 'a running post or two, to run night and day between Edinburgh, in Scotland, and the city of London, to go thither and back in six days;' but the organization of a penny post, for the conveyance of letters and parcels throughout the capital and suburbs, was reserved for the reign of the merry monarch. This beneficial scheme was originated by an upholsterer named Murray, who communicated it to one William Dockwra, a man who for over ten years had laboured with fidelity in the Custom House. Uniting their efforts, they, with great labour and vast expense, carried the plan into execution in the year 1680.

The principal office was stationed at the residence of William Dockwra, in Lime Street ; seven sorting-houses and as many as four hundred receiving-houses were speedily established in the cities of London, Westminster, and the suburbs; and a great number of clerks and messengers were employed to collect, enter, and deliver parcels and letters not exceeding one pound in weight nor ten pounds in value. Stamps were used as an acknowledgment that postage was paid, and likewise to mark the hours when letters were sent out from the offices, by which, in case of delay, its cause might be traced to the messengers; and deliveries took place ten times in the vicinity of the Exchange and Inns of Court, and four times in the suburbs daily. All persons were requested to post their communications before six o'clock in the winter, and seven in the summer, on Saturday nights, 'that the many poor men employed may have a little time to provide for their families against the Lord's Day.' And it was moreover intimated that upon three days at Christmas, and two at Easter and Whitsuntide, as likewise upon the 30th of January, the post would not be delivered.

From the first this scheme promised success, the manner in which it was carried out being wholly admirable; yet there were many who raised their voices against it persistently. Porters and messengers declared it took away their means of subsistence; whilst those of higher grade were confident it was a contrivance of the papists, which enabled them to carry out their wicked schemes with greater security. But these illusions vanished with time; and the penny post became such a success that Government laid claim to it as a branch of the General Post Office, and annexed its revenues to the Crown.*

Another innovation in this interesting reign were stage-coaches, described as affording 'admirable commodiousness both for men and women of better rank, to travel from London and to almost all the villages near this great city, that the like hath not been known in the world, wherein one may be transported to any place, sheltered from foul weather and foul ways, free from endamaging one's health or body by hard jogging or over-violent motion, and this not only at a low price, as about a shilling for every five miles in a day; for the stage-coaches called

---

* In the year 1703 Queen Anne bestowed a grant on Elizabeth, Dowager Countess of Thanet, to erect a penny post-office in Dublin, similar to that in existence in London.

flying coaches make forty or fifty miles in a day, as from London to Cambridge or Oxford, and that in the space of twelve hours, not counting the time for dining, setting forth not too early; nor coming in too late.'

Likewise were divorce suits introduced whilst Charles II. sat upon the throne for the first time—if the case of Henry VIII. be excepted—when my Lord Rosse, in consequence of the misconduct of his lady, had a bill brought into the House of Lords for dissolving his marriage and enabling him to wed again. There being at this period, 1669, a project for divorcing the king from the queen, it was considered Lord Rosse's suit, if successful, would facilitate a like bill in favour of his majesty. After many and stormy debates his lordship gained his case by a majority of two votes. It is worth noting that two of the lords spiritual, Dr. Cosin, Bishop of Durham, and Dr. Wilkins, Bishop of Chester, voted in favour of the bill.

The social history of this remarkable reign would be incomplete without mention of the grace and patronage which Charles II. extended towards the Society of Antiquaries. This learned body, according to Stow, had been in existence since the days of Elizabeth; but for lack of royal acknowledgment of its worth and lore, was permitted to languish in neglect and finally become extinct. However, under the commonwealth the society had revived, from the fact that numbers of the nobility being unemployed in affairs of state, and having no court to attend, applied themselves whilst in retirement to the study of chemistry, mathematics, mechanism, and natural philosophy. The Duke of Devonshire, Marquis of Worcester, Viscount Brouncker, Honourable Robert Boyle, and Sir Robert Murray, built laboratories, made machines, opened mines, and perfected inventions. When the temper of the times permitted, these men, with various others of like tastes, drew together, held weekly meetings at Gresham College in Bishopsgate Street, discoursed on abstruse subjects, and heard erudite lectures, from Dr. Petty on chemistry, from Dr. Wren on astronomy, from Mr. Laurence Rooke on geometry; so that the Society of Antiquaries may be said to have been founded in the last years of the republic.

Now Charles II., having some knowledge

of chemistry and science, looked upon the
society with favourable eyes; and in the first
year of his restoration desired to become one
of its members; expressed satisfaction it had
been placed upon a proper basis in his reign;
represented the difficulty of its labours; suggested certain investigations, and declared his
interest in all its movements. Moreover, in the
year 1662 he bestowed on the society a charter
in which he styled himself its founder and
patron; presented it with a silver mace to be
borne before the president on meeting days; and
gave it the use of the royal arms for a seal. Nor
did his concern for its welfare cease here. He
was frequently present at its meetings, and occasionally witnessed, and assisted 'with his own
hands,' in the performance of experiments. Some
of these were of a singularly interesting character; amongst which may be mentioned infusion of the blood of an animal into the veins
of a man. This took place in the year 1667, the
subject being one Arthur Coga, a minister poor
in worldly substance, who, in exchange for a
guinea, consented to have the operation performed on him. Accordingly two surgeons of

great skill and learning, named Lower and King, on a certain day injected twelve ounces of sheep's blood into his veins. After which he smoked an honest pipe in peace, drank a glass of good canary with relish, and found himself no worse in mind or body. And in two days more fourteen ounces of sheep's blood were substituted for eight of his own without loss of virility to him.

Nor were experiments in vivisection unknown to the Royal Society, as it was called, for the 'Philosophical Transactions' speak of a dog being tied through the back above the spinal artery, thereby depriving him of motion until the artery was loosened, when he recovered; and again, it is recorded that Dr. Charleton cut the spleen out of a living dog with good success.

The weighty discourses of the learned men who constituted the society frequently delighted his majesty; though it must be confessed he sometimes laughed at them, and once sorely puzzled them by asking the following question. 'Supposing,' said Charles, assuming a serious expression, and speaking in a solemn tone, 'two pails of water were placed in two different scales and weighed alike, and that a live bream or small fish was put into one, now why should not the pail in which it was placed weigh heavier than the other?' Most members were troubled to find the king a fitting reply, and many strange theories were advanced by way of explaining why the pail should not be found heavier, none of them being thought satisfactory. But at last a man sitting far down the table was heard to express an opinion, when those surrounding him laughed; hearing which the king, who had not caught his words, asked him to repeat them. 'Why, your majesty,' said he boldly, 'I do believe the pail would weigh heavier.' 'Odds-fish!' cried Charles, bursting out into laughter, 'you are right, my honest fellow!' and so the merriment became general.

The Royal Society was composed of men of quality with a genius for investigation, and men of learning eager for further knowledge. Persons of all nationalities, religions, and professions were admitted members; and it was continually enriched by the addition of curiosities, amongst which in particular were an herb which grew in the stomach of a thrush; the skin of a Moor tanned, with the beard and hair white; a clock, having movements directed by loadstone; an ostrich, whose young had been born alive; mummies; strange fish; and the hearts and livers of vipers. Likewise was the society endowed with gifts, amongst the most notable being the valuable library of Henry Howard, afterwards Duke of Norfolk.

Fostered by this society, science received its first impulse towards the astounding progress it has since achieved. Nay, in this reign the germs of some inventions were sown, which, subsequently springing into existence, have startled the world by their novelty, utility, and power. Monsieur Sorbiere, when in England, was shown a journal kept by Montconis, concerning the transactions of the Royal Society, in which several new devices, 'which scarce can be believed unless seen,' were described. Amongst these were an instrument for showing alterations in the weather, whether from heat, cold, wind, or rain; a method for blowing up ships; a process for purifying salt water, so that it could be drunk; and an instrument by which those ignorant of drawing could sketch and design any object.

He also states Dr. Wallis had taught one born deaf and dumb to read.

In 1663, 'the right honourable (and deservedly to be praised and admired) Edward Somerset, Marquis of Worcester,' published a quaint volume entitled ' A Century of the Names and Scantlings of such Inventions as at present I can call to mind to have tried and perfected, which (my former notes being lost) I have, at the instance of a powerful friend, endeavoured to set down in such a way as may sufficiently instruct me to put any of them in practice.' Amongst these are enumerated false decks, such as in a moment should kill and take prisoners as many as should board the ship, without blowing her up, and in a quarter of an hour's time should recover their former shape without discovering the secret; a portable fortification, able to contain five hundred men, which in the space of six hours might be set up, and made cannon-proof; a dexterous tinder-box which served as a pistol, and was yet capable of lighting a fire or candle at any hour of the night without giving its possessor the trouble of stretching his hand from bed; a lock, the ways of opening which might be varied ten millions of times, but which on a stranger touching it would cause an alarm that could not be stopped, and would register what moneys had been taken from its keeping; a boat which would work against wind and tide; with various other discoveries to the number of one hundred, all arrived at from mathematical studies.

The means of propelling a boat against such disadvantages, to which the Marquis of Worcester alludes, was in all probability by steam-power. This he described as 'an admirable and most forcible way to drive up water by fire,' the secret of which he is believed to have first discovered.* In the preface to his little book, the marquis states he had sacrificed from six to seven hundred thousand pounds in bringing his various inventions to perfection; after which it is satisfactory to find he derived some profit from one of them, conceived, as he says, 'by heavenly inspiration.' This was a water-engine for drying marsh-lands and mines, requiring

* Before the century was concluded, Captain Savery contrived a steam-engine which was certainly the first put to practical uses. It has been stated that he owed the knowledge of this invention to hints conveyed in Lord Worcester's little volume.

neither pump, suckers, barrels, bellows, nor external nor additional help, save that afforded from its own operations. This engine Sorbiere describes as one of the most curious things he had a mind to see, and says one man by the help of this machine raised four large buckets full of water in an instant forty feet high, through a pipe eight inches long. An act of parliament was passed enabling the marquis to reap the benefit and profit from this invention, subject to a tenth part which was reserved for the king and his heirs.

The Royal Society soon became one of the foremost objects of interest in the city. Foreigners of distinction were conducted to its rooms that they might behold the visible signs of knowledge it could proudly boast; and women of culture were admitted to hear the lectures its members delivered.

Amongst these latter may be mentioned the eccentric Duchess of Newcastle; a lady who dressed her footmen in velvet coats, habited herself in antique gowns, wrote volumes of plays and poetry, desired the reputation of learning, and indulged in circumstances of pomp and state. Having expressed her desire to be present at one of the meetings of the Royal Society, the council prepared to receive her, not, it must be admitted, without some fear her extravagance would expose them to the ridicule of the town, and place them at the mercy of ballad-mongers. So it happened one fair Mayday, in the year 1667, a vast concourse of people had assembled to witness her arrival at Arundel House in the Strand, where the society held its meetings for some years after the burning of Gresham College. And she in good time reaching there, surrounded by her maids of honour, gentlemen in waiting, and lackeys, was met by the president, Viscount Brouncker, having his mace carried before him, and was conducted to the great room. When the meeting was over, various experiments were tried for her satisfaction; amongst others a piece of roasted mutton was turned into pure blood. The while she witnessed these sights, crowds of gallants gathered round her that they might catch and retain such fine things as fell from her lips; but she only cried out her wonder and admiration at all she saw; and at the end of her visit was conducted in state to her coach by several noble lords, notable amongst whom was a vastly pretty young man, Francis Seymour, fifth Duke of Somerset.

CHAPTER X.

A period rich in literature.—John Milton's early life.--Writing 'Paradise Lost.'—Its publication and success.—His later works and death.—John Dryden gossips with wits and players.—Lord Rochester's revenge.—Elkanah Settle.—John Crowne.—Thomas Otway rich in miseries. Dryden assailed by villains.—The ingenious Abraham Cowley.—The author of 'Hudibras.'—Young Will Wycherley and Lady Castlemaine.—The story of his marriage.—Andrew Marvell, poet and politician.—John Bunyan.

THE men of genius who lived in the days of the merry monarch have rendered his reign, like that of Elizabeth, illustrious in the annals of literature. The fact of 'Paradise Lost,' the 'Pilgrim's Progress,' 'Hudibras' and 'Alexander's Feast' being given to the world whilst Charles II. occupied the throne, would have sufficiently marked the epoch as one exceeding in intellectual brilliancy; but besides these works, an abundance of plays, poems, satires, treatises, and histories added fresh lustre to this remarkable period.

At the period of the restoration, John Milton had reached his fifty-second year. He had studied in the University of Cambridge; published the 'Masque of Comus;' likewise a treatise against the Established Church; taught school at Aldersgate Street; married a wife and advocated divorce; printed a pamphlet to compose the minds of those disturbed by the murder of Charles I.; as also a defence of his murderers, justifying the monarch's execution, for which the author was awarded a thousand pounds; had become secretary to Cromwell, whom he stooped to flatter*; and had even, on the advent of his

* 'To your virtue,' writes John Milton to Oliver Cromwell, 'overpowering and resistless, every man gives way, except some who, without equal qualifications, aspire to equal honours, who envy the distinctions of merit greater than their own, and who have yet to learn that, in the coalition of human society, nothing is more pleasing to God, or more agreeable to reason, than that the highest mind should have the sovereign power. Such, sir, are you by general confession: such are the things achieved by you, the greatest and most glorious of our countrymen, the director of our public councils, the leader of unconquered armies, the father of your country; for by that title does every good man hail you with sincere and voluntary praise.'

majesty's return, written and set forth 'A Ready and Easy Way to establish a Free Commonwealth.'

On the landing of Charles II. Milton withdrew to the privacy afforded by a residence in Bartholomew Close, near West Smithfield. For a time he was apprehensive of punishment. His pamphlet justifying the late king's execution was, with others of a like kind, burned by the common hangman; but though parliament ordered the attorney-general would prosecute the authors of these works, Milton was neither seized nor brought to trial. Soon after his arrival, Charles published an act of grace promising free pardon to those instrumental in overthrowing his father's government, with the exception of such as had contrived his death; and inasmuch as Milton had but justified that monstrous act after it had taken place, he escaped condemnation. Moreover, he received a special pardon, which passed the privy seal in December, 1660. His escape has been attributed to his friend Davenant. This loyal soldier had, when taken by Cromwell's troopers in the civil war, been condemned to speedy death; from which, by Milton's intercession, he escaped; an act of mercy Davenant now repaid in kind, by appealing to his friends in behalf of the republican's safety.

Having secured his freedom, Milton lived in peace and obscurity in Jewin Street, near Aldersgate Street. During the commonwealth his first wife, the mother of his three children, had died; on which he sought solace and companionship in a union with Catherine Woodcock, who survived her marriage but twelve months; and being left free once more, he, in the year of grace 1661, entered into the bonds of holy matrimony for a third time, with Elizabeth Minshul, a lady of excellent family and shrewish temper, who rendered his daughters miserable in their father's lifetime, and defrauded them after his death.

In order to support his family he continued to keep a school, and likewise employed himself in writing 'Paradise Lost,' the composition of which he had begun five years previously. From his youth upwards he had been ambitious to furnish the world with some important work; and prevision of resulting fame had given him strength and fortitude in periods of difficulty and depression. And now the time had arrived for realization of his dream, though stricken by blindness, harassed by an unquiet wife, and threatened by poverty, he laboured sore for fame. The more fully to enjoy quiet necessary to his mental condition, he removed to a house in Artillery Walk, Bunhill Fields. His life was one of simplicity. He rose as early as four o'clock in summer and five in winter, and being 'smit with the love of sacred song,' had a chapter of the Bible read to him; studied until twelve, dined frugally at one, and afterwards held discourse with such friends as came to visit him.

One of these was Thomas Elwood, a quaker much esteemed amongst good men, who, in order that he might enjoy the advantages of the poet's conversation, read Latin to him every afternoon save Sunday. The whilst his voice rose and fell in regular monotony, the blind man drank his words with thirsty ears; and so acute were the senses remaining to him, that when Elwood read what he did not understand, Milton perceived it from the inflection of his voice, and stopped him to explain the passage.

In fair weather the poet wandered abroad, enjoying the fragrance of sweet pasture land, and the warmth of glad sunlight he might not behold. And anon, seated in a high-backed chair without his door, his straight pale face full of repose and dignity, his light brown hair falling in curls upon his shoulders, his large grey eyes, 'clear to outward view of blemish or of spot,' fixed on vacancy, his figure clad in coarse cloth—he received those who sought his society.

In their absence the poet spent solitary hours conning over as many lines of the great poem as his memory could store, until one of his friends arrived, and relieved him by taking the stanzas down. Frequently his nephew, Edward Philips, performed this task for him. To him Milton was in the habit of showing his work as it advanced, and Philips states he found it frequently required correction in orthography and punctuation, by reason of the various hands which had written it. As summer advanced, he was no longer favoured by a sight of the poem; inquiring the reason of which, Milton told him 'his vein never happily flowed but from the autumnal equinox to the vernal; and that whatever he attempted at other times was never to his satisfaction, though he courted his fancy never so much.'

In the year 1665 'Paradise Lost' was completed, but no steps were taken towards its publication, as the author, in company with his neighbours, fled from the dreaded plague. The following year the citizens were harassed by losses sustained from the great fire, so that Milton did not seek to dispose of his poem until 1667; when, on the 27th of April, it was sold to Samuel Simmons, a publisher residing in Aldersgate Street. The agreement entered into stated Milton should receive an immediate payment of five pounds, with the stipulation that he should be given an equal sum on sale of thirteen hundred copies of the first edition, and five pounds on disposal of the same number of the second edition, and yet five pounds more after another such sale of the third edition. Each edition was to number fifteen hundred books. Two years after the publication of 'Paradise Lost,' its author received the second payment of five pounds; five years later a third payment was made him; before the fourth fell due his life had been set free from care.

From the first his poem had come in contact with a few receptive minds, and borne the blessed fruit of appreciation. Richardson recounts that Sir John Denham, a poet and man of culture, one morning brought a sheet of the great epic fresh from the press to his friend Sir George Hungerford. 'Why, what have you there?' asked the latter. 'Part of the noblest poem that was ever written in any language or in any age,' said Sir John, as he laid the pages before him. And a few weeks later my Lord Dorset, looking over a bookstall in Little Britain, found a copy of this work, which he opened carelessly at first, until he met some passages which struck him with surprise and filled him with admiration: observing which the honest bookseller besought him to speak in favour of the poem, for it lay upon his hands like so much waste-paper. My lord bought a copy, carried it home, read and sent it to Dryden, who, in due time returning the volume, expressed his opinion of its merits in flattering terms. 'The author,' said he, 'cuts us all out—aye, even the ancients too.'

Such instances as these were, however, few in number. That the work did not meet with wider appreciation and quicker sale is not surprising when it is called to mind that from 1623 to 1664 but two editions of Shakespeare's works, comprising in all about one thousand copies, had been printed. In an age when learning was by no means universal, and polite reading uncommon, it was indeed a source of congratulation, rather than a topic for commiseration, that the work of a republican had in two years reached a sale of thirteen hundred copies.

Before a third edition was required his fame had spread. The house in which he had been born, in Bread Street, was shown with pride to foreign visitors; parents sent their sons to read to him, that they might reap the benefit of his remarks. The latter testimony to his genius was a tribute the blind poet appreciated. But it happened there were times and seasons when these obliging youths were not at hand, or when it was inconvenient for him to receive them. On such occasions he demanded that his daughters should read him the books he required, though these were frequently written in Hebrew,

Greek, Latin, Italian, and Spanish—languages of which they were wholly ignorant. The torment this inflicted on those striving to pronounce unaccustomed words which had no meaning to their ears, and the torture endured by him, may readily be conceived. Expressions of complaint on the one side, and of pain on the other, continually interrupted the readings, which were eventually wholly abandoned; the poet sending his children, whose education was so limited that they were unable to write, to learn 'ingenious sorts of manufacture proper for women, particularly embroideries in gold and silver.'

When in 1665 Milton had shown his poem to Elwood, the good quaker observed, ' Thou hast said a great deal upon Paradise Lost: what hast thou to say upon Paradise Found?' This question resting in the poet's mind, in due time produced fruit; for no sooner had his first poem been published than he set about composing the latter, which, under the name of ' Paradise Regained,' was given to the world in 1670. ' This,' said he to Elwood, ' is owing to you; for you put it into my head by the question which you put to me, which otherwise I had not thought of.' This poem, he believed, had merits far superior to those of 'Paradise Lost,' which he could not bear to hear praised in preference to 'Paradise Regained.' In the same year he published 'Samson Agonistes,' and two years later a treatise on 'Logic,' and another on 'True Religion, Heresy, Schism, Toleration, and the Best Methods to Prevent the Growth of Popery.' In this, the mind which had soared to heaven and descended to hell in its boundless flight, argues that catholics should not be allowed the right of public or private worship. In the last year of his life he republished his 'Juvenile Poems,' together with 'Familiar Epistles in Latin.'

He had now reached his sixty-sixth year. His life had been saddened by blindness, his health enfeebled by illness, his domesticity troubled by his first marriage and his last, his desires disappointed by the result of political events. So that when, on the 10th of November, 1674, death summoned him, he departed without regret.

Amongst those who visited Milton was John Dryden, whom the author of 'Paradise Lost' regarded as 'a good rhymester, but no poet,' an opinion with which posterity has not held. At the restoration, John Dryden was in his twenty-ninth year. The son of Sir Erasmus Dryden, Baronet, of Canons Ashby, he enjoyed an income of two hundred pounds a year, a sum then considered sufficient to defray the expenses of a young man of good breeding. He had passed through Westminster School, taken a degree at Cambridge, written a eulogistic stanza on the death of Cromwell, and a joyous poem on the happy restoration of the merry monarch.

Three years after the arrival of his majesty, Dryden's comedy entitled 'The Wild Gallant' was produced, this being the first of twenty-eight plays which followed. In the year 1668 he had the honour to succeed Sir William Davenant as poet laureate, the salary attached to which office was one hundred pounds a year and a tierce of wine. His dignity was moreover enhanced, though his happiness was by no means increased, by his marriage with the Lady Elizabeth Howard, daughter of the Earl of Berkshire. For my lady's temper sorely marred the poet's peace, and left such impressions upon his mind, that to the end of his days his invectives against the bonds of matrimony were bitter and deep. In justice it must be mentioned the Lady Elizabeth's mental condition was supposed to be unsettled; a conjecture which was proved true by a madness which befell her, subsequent to her husband's death.

Dryden was now a well-known figure in town, consorting with men of the highest quality and parts, and gossiping with wits and players who frequented Will's coffee-house. Here, indeed, a special chair was appropriated to his use; which being placed by the fire in winter, and on the balcony in summer, he was pleased to designate as his winter and his summer seat. At Will's he was wont to hold forth on the ingenuity of his plays, the perfection of his poems, and the truth of astrology. It was whilst leaving this coffee-house one night a memorable occurrence befell the poet, of which more anon.

It happened at one time the brilliant, poetical, and mercurial Earl of Rochester extended his favour and friendship towards Dryden, gratified by which, the poet had, after the manner of those days, dedicated a play to him, 'Marriage a la Mode.' This favour his lordship received with graciousness, and no doubt repaid with liberality. After a while, Dryden, led by choice or interest, sought a new patron in the person of the Earl of Mulgrave. For this nobleman Rochester had long entertained a bitter animosity, which had arisen from rivalry, and had been intensified from the fact that Rochester, refusing to fight him, had been branded as a coward. Not daring to attack the peer, Rochester resolved to avenge himself upon the poet. In order to effect his humiliation, the earl at once bestowed his favour on Elkanah Settle, a playwright and poet of mean abilities. He had originally been master of a puppet-show, had written verses to order for city pageants, and produced a tragedy in heroic verse, entitled 'Cambyses, King of Persia.'

His patron being at this time in favour with the king, introduced Settle to the notice of the court, and induced the courtiers to play his second tragedy, 'The Empress of Morocco,' at Whitehall, before their majesties. This honour, which Dryden, though poet laureate, had never received, gave Elkanah Settle unmerited notoriety; the benefit of which was apparent by the applause his tragedy received when subsequently produced at the Duke's Theatre in Dorset Gardens. Nor did the honour and profit which 'The Empress of Morocco' brought him end here; it was published by William Cademan, and had the distinction of being the first English play ever illustrated, or sold for the price of two shillings. It was scarce to be expected, in an age when men ventilated their merest grievances by the publication of pamphlets, Dryden could refrain from pointing out to the public the mistake into which they had fallen by honouring this man. Nor was he singular in his feelings of animosity. The poets Shadwell and Crowne, believing themselves ignored and neglected, whilst their rival was enriched and exalted, joined Dryden in writing a merciless criticism upon Settle's tragedy. This was entitled ' The Empress of Morocco, or some few erratas to be printed instead of the sculptures,* with the second edition of the play.' In

* Illustrations.

this Settle was described as 'an animal of a most deplored intellect, without reading and understanding ;' whilst his play was characterized as 'a tale told by an idiot, full of noise and fury signifying nothing.' To these remarks and others of like quality, Settle replied in the same strain, so that the quarrel diverted the town and even disturbed the quiet of the universities. Time did ample justice to both men; lowering Settle to play the part of a dragon in a booth at Bartholomew Fair, and consecrating Dryden to immortality.

Before the clamour resulting from this dispute had ended, Rochester, fickle and eccentric, grew weary of his *protégé*, and consequently abandoned him. He had not, however, tired of humiliating the laureate, and to mortify him the more, introduced a new poet at court. This was John Crowne, a man then little known to the town, and now best remembered as author of 'Sir Courtly Nice,' a comedy of wit and entertainment. So well did he succeed in obtaining favour at court, through Rochester's influence, that the queen ordered him to write a masque. This command he immediately obeyed, pro-

LADY CASTLEMAINE, DUCHESS OF CLEVELAND.

ducing 'Calisto, or the Chaste Nymph,' which was acted at Whitehall by the Duke of York's fair daughters, the Princesses Mary and Anne, together with many gracious ladies and noble lords. Dryden, probably the better to hide the mortification he felt at seeing his office as laureate unceremoniously usurped, offered to write an epilogue for the occasion; but this service was, through Rochester's interference, rejected. The masque proved a brilliant success; 'the dancing, singing, and music, which were all in the highest perfection, and the graceful action, incomparable beauty, and splendid habits of those ladies who accompanied them, afforded the spectators extraordinary delight.' 'Calisto' was therefore performed thirty times.

The author's gratitude for his lordship's patronage was only equalled by his disappointment upon its hasty withdrawal. Growing weary of him, Rochester found a more worthy object for his favour in Thomas Otway, a poet rich in all the miseries which afflicted genius in those days. Son of the rector of Woolbeding, pupil at Winchester School, and commoner of Christchurch, Cambridge, he had on his arrival in town vainly sought employment as an actor, and barely earned bread as a play-writer. Before he became a *protégé* of my Lord Rochester he had written 'Alcibiades,' a tragedy, he being then, in 1665, in his twenty-fifth year. His next play was 'Don Carlos, Prince of Spain,' which, through the earl's influence, gained great success. In the preface to this tragedy he acknowledges his unspeakable obligations to my lord, who he says made it his business to establish 'Don Carlos' in the good opinion of the king and of his royal highness the Duke of York. Unwarned by the fate of his predecessors, and heedless of the fickleness of his patron, he basked in hope in the present, mercifully unconscious of the cruel death by starvation which awaited him in the future. Alas! Rochester not only forsook him, but loaded him with satire in a poem entitled 'Session of the Poets.'

In verses which he wrote soon after, entitled 'An Allusion to the Tenth Satire,' Rochester likewise attacked Dryden; who, in the preface of his 'All for Love,' replied in like manner. Then there appeared an 'Essay on Satire,' which ridiculed the king, dealt severely with his mistresses, said uncivil things of the courtiers in general, and of my Lord Rochester in particular. The noble earl was indeed described as being 'lewd in every limb,' affected in his wit, mean in his actions, and cowardly in his disposition. Now, though this was conceived and brought forth by my Lord Mulgrave, Rochester suspected Dryden of its authorship, and resolved to punish him forthwith. Accordingly, on the night of the 18th of December, 1679, when Dryden was passing through Rose Street, Covent Garden, on his homeward way from Will's Coffee House, he was waylaid by some ruffians, and, before he could draw his sword, promptly surrounded and severely beaten.

This occurrence caused considerable sensation throughout the town, and though surmises arose in many minds as to who had hired the bravoes, it was found impossible to prove them. In hope of gaining some clue to the instigator of the attack, Dryden caused the following advertisement to be inserted in the *London Gazette* and *Domestic Intelligence* for three consecutive days: 'Whereas John Dryden, Esq., was on Monday, the 18th instant, at night, barbarously assaulted and wounded in Rose Street, in Covent Garden, by divers men unknown; if any person shall make discovery of the said offenders to the said Mr. Dryden, or to any justice of the peace, he shall not only receive fifty pounds, which is deposited in the hands of Mr. Blanchard Goldsmith, next door to Temple Bar, for the said purpose; but if he be a principal or an accessory in the said fact, his majesty is graciously pleased to promise him his pardon for the same.'

Dryden sought no opportunity for revenge; for which restraint, outliving Rochester, and having a noble mind and generous disposition, he was no doubt glad at heart. Not only did he survive the earl, but likewise the king. To the company and conversation of that gracious sovereign the poet was frequently admitted, a privilege which resulted in satisfaction and pleasure to both. One pleasant day towards the end of his majesty's reign, whilst they walked in the Mall, Charles said to him, 'If I were a poet, and indeed I think I am poor enough to be one, I would write a satire on sedition.' Taking this hint, Dryden speedily set himself to work, and brought a poem on such a subject to his royal master, who rewarded him with a hundred broad pieces.

Amongst Dryden's friends was the excellent and ingenious Abraham Cowley, whose youth had given the promise of distinction his manhood fulfilled. It is related that when quite a lad, he found in the window recess of his mother's apartment a copy of Spenser's 'Faerie Queene.' Opening the book, he read it with delight, and his receptive mind reflecting the poet's fire, he resolved likewise to exercise the art of poesy. In 1628, when at the age of ten, he wrote the 'The Tragic History of Pyramus and Thisbe;' five years later he published a volume of poems; and whilst yet a schoolboy wrote his pastoral comedy, 'Love's Riddle.'

When at St. John's College, Oxford, he gave proof of his loyalty by writing a poem entitled the 'Puritan and the Papist,' which gained him the friendship of courtiers. On the Queen of Charles I. taking refuge in France, he soon followed her, and becoming secretary to the Earl of St. Albans, conducted the correspondence between her majesty and the king, ciphering and deciphering their letters, and such as were sent or received by those immediately concerned in the cause of royalty. In this situation he remained until four years previous to the restoration, when he was sent into England for the purpose of observing the condition of the nation, and reporting the same. Scarce had he set foot in London when he was seized, examined, and only liberated on a friend offering bail for him to the amount of one thousand pounds.

The better to disguise the object of his visit, and lull suspicions of republicans, he took out the degree of Doctor of Physic at Oxford; after which he retired into Kent, where he devoted a great portion of his time to the study of botany and the composition of poetry. On Cromwell's death he hastened to France, and remained there until the king's return; which he celebrated by a song of triumph. Like hundreds of others who had served Charles in his exile, he looked forward to gratitude and reward, but met disappointment and neglect. Amongst the numerous places and employments the change of government opened in court and state, not one was offered the loyal poet.

Nay, his hardships did not end here; for having, in 1663, produced his merry comedy, 'Cutter of Coleman Street,' it was treated with severity as a censure upon the king. Feeling over-nervous to witness the result of its first representation, the poet absented himself from the playhouse; but thither his friends Dryden and Sprat sped, hoping they might be able to bear him tidings of its triumph. When they returned to him at night and told him of its fate, 'he received the news of its ill success,' says Sprat, 'not with so much firmness as might have been expected from so great a man.' Of all intent to satirize the king he was entirely innocent—a fact he set before the public in the preface to his play on its publication. Having, he argues, followed the fallen fortunes of the royal family so long, it was unlikely he would select the time of their restoration to quarrel with them.

Feeling his grievances acutely, he now published a poem called 'The Complaint,' which met with but little success; whereon, depressed by ill-fortune and disgusted by ingratitude, he sought consolation in the peace of a country life.

Through the influence of his old friend, Lord St. Albans, and the Duke of Buckingham, he obtained a lease of the queen's lands at Chertsey, which produced him an income of about three hundred pounds a year—a sum sufficient for his few wants and moderate desires. He resided here but two years, when he died, on the 28th of July, 1667. Milton, on hearing of his death, was troubled. The three greatest English poets, he declared, were Spenser, Shakespeare, and Cowley.

The ungrateful neglect with which he was treated in life was sought to be atoned for by useless honours paid him after death. His remains were first conveyed to Wallingford House, then a residence of the Duke of Buckingham, from whence they were carried in a coach drawn by six horses, and followed by all the men of letters and wits of the town, divers stately bishops, courtiers, and men of quality, whose carriages exceeded one hundred in number, to Westminster Abbey. Here the poet was laid at rest beside Geoffrey Chaucer, and not far removed from gentle Spenser, whose words had first inspired his happy muse.

The literary wealth of this reign was furthermore enhanced by the genius of Butler, the inimitable author of 'Hudibras,' concerning whom little is known, save that he was born in 1612, and spent his life in poverty. He passed some years as clerk to a justice of the peace; he also served a great man's steward, and acted as secretary to Sir Samuel Luke, one of Cromwell's officers. With those of the commonwealth he held no part; that he was a royalist at heart his great satire indicates. The first part of this was published in the third year of the restoration, and was introduced to the notice of his majesty by my Lord Dorset. So delighted was the monarch by its wit that its lines were continually on his lips, an example speedily followed by the courtiers. It was considered certain a man possessing such brilliant genius and loyal nature would be rewarded with place or pension; but neither boon was bestowed upon him. Resting his hopes on future achievements, the second part of 'Hudibras' appeared in 1664; but again his recompense was delayed. Clarendon made him promises of valuable employments, which were never fulfilled; and to soothe his disappointment the king sent him a present of three hundred guineas.

Indignant at the neglect from which he suffered, his friend Wycherley spoke to the Duke of Buckingham on his behalf, saying it was a shame to the court a man of Butler's parts should be allowed to suffer want. With this his grace readily agreed, and promised to use his influence towards remedying the poet's illfortune; but time went by, and his condition remained unaltered. Whereon Wycherley conceived the idea of bringing Butler and the duke together, that the latter might the more certainly remember him. He therefore succeeded in making his grace name an hour and place in which they might meet. So it came to pass they were together one day at the Roebuck Tavern; but scarce had Buckingham opened his lips when a pimp of his acquaintance—' the creature was likewise a knight '—passed by with a couple of ladies. To a man of Buckingham's character the temptation was too seductive to be neglected; accordingly, he darted after those who allured him, leaving the needy poet, whom he saw no more. Butler lived until 1680, dying in poverty. Longueville, having in vain solicited a subscription to defray the expenses of the poet's burial in Westminster Abbey, laid him to rest in the churchyard of Covent Garden.

Wycherley, the friend of Butler, though a child of the Muses, was superior to poverty. He was born in the year of grace 1640, and early in life sent for his better education into France. Returning to England soon after the king had come unto his own, young Wycherley entered Queen's College, Oxford, from whence he departed without obtaining a degree. He then betook himself to town, and became a law student. The Temple, however, had less attraction for him than the playhouse. Indeed, before leaving Oxford he had written a couple of comedies—to wit, 'Love in a Wood,' and 'The Gentleman Dancing Master,' a fact entitling him to be considered a man of parts. Not satisfied with this distinction, he soon developed tastes for pleasures of the town, and became a man of fashion. His wit illuminated choice gatherings of congenial spirits at coffee-houses; his epigrams were repeated by boon companions in the precincts of the court.

In the year 1672 his comedy 'Love in a Wood' was produced. It immediately gained universal favour, and, moreover, speedily attracted the attention of his majesty's mistress, the Duchess of Cleveland. Wycherley was a man well to look upon: her grace was a lady eager for adventure. Desiring his acquaintance, and impatient of delay, she introduced herself to his notice in a manner eminently characteristic of the age. It happened when driving one day through Pall Mall, she encountered Wycherley riding in his coach in an opposite direction. Thrusting her head out of the window of her vehicle, she saluted the author with a title unknown to the conversations of polite society in the present day.

The fashionable playwright understanding the motive which prompted her remark, hastily ordered his coach to follow hers; and, overtaking her, uncovered and began a speech becoming so ardent a gallant.

'Madam,' said he, 'you have been pleased to bestow a title on me which belongs only to the fortunate. Will your ladyship be at the play to-night?'

'Well,' replied her grace, well pleased at this beginning, ' what if I am there ?'

'Why, then,' answered he, 'I will be there to wait on your ladyship, though I disappoint a fine woman who has made me an assignation.'

'So,' said this frail daughter of Eve, greedily swallowing his flattery, 'you are sure to disappoint a woman who has favoured you for one who has not ?'

'Yes,' quoth he, readily enough, 'if the one who has not favoured me is the finer woman of the two. But he who can be constant to your ladyship till he can find a finer, is sure to die your captive.'

That night her grace sat in the front row of the king's box at Drury Lane playhouse, and sure enough there was handsome Will Wycherley sitting in the pit underneath. The gentleman cast his eyes upwards and sighed; the lady looked down and played with her fan; after which preliminaries they fell into conversation which both found far more interesting than the comedy then being enacted before their eyes. This was the beginning of an intimacy concerning which the court made merry, and of which the town spoke scandal. My lady disguised herself as a country wench, and visited his chambers. Mr. Wycherley dedicated his play, 'Love in a Wood,' to her in elegant phraseology. He was of opinion that she stood as little in need of flattery as her beauty did of art; he was anxious to let the world know he was the greatest admirer she had; and he was desirous of returning her his grateful acknowledgment for the favours he had received from her.

The interest of this romance was presently intensified by the introduction of a rival in the person of the Duke of Buckingham. Probably from fear an intrigue with such a prominent figure would, if indulged in, quickly become known to the king, she refused to encourage Buckingham's love. His grace was not only a passionate lover, but likewise a revengeful man; accordingly, he resolved to punish my lady for her lack of good taste. It therefore became his habit to speak of her intrigues before the court, and to name the individuals who received her favours. Now Wycherley, being amongst these, grew fearful his amour with the duchess should become known to the king, from whom at this time he expected an appointment. Accordingly, he besought his good friends, Lord Rochester and Sir Charles Sedley, to remonstrate on his behalf with the duke. These gentlemen undertook that kindly office, and in order to make the rivals acquainted, besought his grace to sup with the playwright. The duke, complying with their request, met Wycherley in a friendly spirit, and soon professed himself delighted with his wit; nay, before the feast was over he drank his health in a bumper of red wine, and declared himself Mr. Wycherley's very good friend and faithful servant henceforth.

Moreover, he was as good as his word; for, being master of the horse, he soon after appointed Wycherley an equerry, and subsequently gave him a commission as captain of a regiment of which he was colonel. Nor did the duke's services to the dramatist end here; for when occasion offered he introduced him to the merry monarch, and so pleased was the king with the author's conversational powers that he admitted him to his friendship. His majesty's regard for Wycherley gradually ripened, and once when he lay ill of fever at his lodgings in Bow Street,

Covent Garden, the merry monarch visited him, cheered him with words of kindness, and promised he would send him to Montpelier when he was well enough to travel. For this good purpose Charles sent him five hundred pounds, and Wycherley spent the winter of 1679 abroad.

Previous to this date he had written, besides his first comedy, three others which had been received with great favour by the town, viz., 'The Gentleman Dancing Master,' 'The Country Wife,' and 'The Plain Dealer.' Soon after his return to England the crisis of his life arrived, and he married. His introduction to the lady whom fate ordained to become his wife is not the least singular episode in a remarkable biography. Being at Tunbridge Wells, then a place of fashion and liberty, he was one day walking with a friend named Fairbeard. And it happened as they were passing a book-stall they overheard a gentlewoman inquire for the 'Plain Dealer.'

'Madam,' says Mr. Fairbeard, uncovering, 'since you are for the "Plain Dealer," there he is for you;' whereon he led Wycherley towards her.

'This lady,' says that gentleman, making her a profound bow, 'can bear plain speaking; for she appears to be so accomplished, that what would be compliment said to others, spoken to her would be plain dealing.'

'No truly, sir,' replied the lady; 'I am not without my faults, like the rest of my sex; and yet, notwithstanding all my faults, I love plain dealing, and never am more fond of it than when it points out my errors.'

'Then, madam,' said Mr. Fairbeard, 'you and the plain dealer seem designed by heaven for each other.'

These pretty speeches having been delivered and received with every mark of civility, Mr. Wycherley made his exit with the lady, who was none other than the Countess of Drogheda, a young widow gifted with beauty and endowed by fortune. Day by day he waited on her at her lodging, accompanied her in her walks, and attended her to the assemblies. Finally, when she returned to town he married her. It is sad yet true the union did not result in perfect happiness. Mr. Wycherley had a reputation for gallantry, the Countess of Drogheda was the victim of suspicion. Knowing jealousy is begot by love, and mindful of sacrifices she had made in marrying him, Wycherley behaved towards her with much kindness. In compliance with her wishes he desisted visiting the court, a place she probably knew from experience was rife with temptation; and moreover when he cracked a bottle of wine with convivial friends at the Cock Tavern, opposite his lodgings in Bow Street, he, for the greater satisfaction of his wife, would leave the windows open of the room in which he sat, that she might from the vantage ground of her home see there were no hussies in the company.

As proof of her love, she, when dying, settled her fortune upon him; but unhappily his just right was disputed by her family. The case therefore went into litigation, for the expenses of which, together with other debts, Wycherley was cast into prison. Here the brilliant wit, clever writer, and boon companion, was allowed to remain seven long years. When released from this vile bondage, another king than the merry monarch occupied the English throne.

The name of Andrew Marvell is inseparably

connected with this period. He was born in the year 1620 in the town of Kingston-upon-Hull; his father being a clever schoolmaster, worthy minister, and 'an excellent preacher, who never broached what he had never brewed, but that which he had studied some compitent time before.' At the age of fifteen, Andrew Marvell was sent to Trinity College, Cambridge. But he had not long been there when he withdrew himself, lured, as some authorities state, by wiles of the wicked Jesuits; repulsed, as others say, by severities of the head of his college. Leaving the university, he set out for London, where his father, who hastened thither in search of him, found him examining some old volumes on a bookstall. He was prevailed to return to his college, where, in 1638, he took his degree as bachelor of arts.

On the completion of his studies and death of his father, he travelled through Holland, France, and Italy. Whilst abroad he began to produce those satirical verses such as were destined to render him famous. One of his earliest efforts in this direction was aimed at the Abbé de Maniban, a learned ecclesiastic, whose chief fault in Marvell's eyes lay in the fact of his professing to judge characters from handwriting.

Whilst in Italy, Andrew Marvell met John Milton, and they having many tastes and convictions in common, became fast friends. In 1653, the former returned to England, and for some time acted as tutor to Mistress Fairfax; he being an excellent scholar, and a great master of the Latin tongue. He now led a peaceful and obscure life until 1657. In that year, Milton, 'laying aside,' as he wrote, 'those jealousies, and that emulation which mine own condition might suggest to me,' introduced him to Bradshaw; soon after which he was made assistant-secretary to Milton, who was then in the service of Cromwell.

He had not been long engaged in this capacity, when the usurper died; and Marvell's occupation being gone, the goodly burgesses of the town of Hull, who loved him well, elected him as their representative in parliament, for which service, in accordance with a custom of the time, he was paid. The salary, it is true, was not large, amounting to two shillings a day for borough members; yet when kindly feeling and honest satisfaction mutually existed between elector and representative, as in Marvell's case, the wage was at times supplemented by such acceptable additions as home-cured pork and home-brewed ale. 'We must first give you thanks,' wrote Marvell on one occasion to his constituents, on the receipt of a cask of beer, 'for the kind present you have pleased to send us, which will give occasion to us to remember you often; but the quantity is so great, that it might make sober men forgetful.'

He now, in the warfare of political life, made free use of his keen wit and bitter sarcasm as serviceable weapons. These were chiefly employed in exposing measures he considered calculated to ruin the country, though they might gratify the king. However, he had no hatred of monarchy, but would occasionally divert Charles by the sharpness of his satire and brilliancy of his wit. Considering how valuable these would be if employed in service of the court, Charles resolved to tempt Marvell's integrity. For this purpose the Lord Treasurer Danby sought and found him in his chamber, situated in the second floor of a mean house standing in a court off the Strand. Groping his way up the dark and narrow staircase of the domicile, the great minister stumbled, and falling against a door, was precipitated into Marvell's apartment, head foremost. Surprised at his appearance, the satirist asked my Lord Danby if he had not mistaken his way. 'No,' said the courtier with a bow 'not since I have found Mr. Marvell.' He then proceeded to tell him that the king, being impressed by a high sense of his abilities, was desirous of serving him. Apprehending what services were expected in return, Marvell answered that he who accepted favours from the court was bound to vote in its interests. 'Nay,' said my lord, 'his majesty but desires to know if there is any place at court you would accept.' On which Marvell replied he could receive nothing with honour, for either he must treat the king with ingratitude by refusing compliance with court measures, or be a traitor to his country by yielding to them. The only favour he therefore begged was, that his majesty would esteem him a loyal subject; the truer to his interests in refusing his offers than he would be by accepting them. It is stated that Lord Danby, surprised at so much purity in an age of corruption, furthermore tempted him with a bag of gold, which Marvell obstinately refused to accept.

He died suddenly in the year 1678, leaving behind him a reputation for humour and satire which has rarely been excelled.

Besides these poets and dramatists, there were other great men, who as prose writers, helped to render the literary history of the period remarkable for its brilliancy. Amongst these were Lord Clarendon, High Chancellor of England, concerning whom much has already been said; and Thomas Hobbs of Malmesbury, better known as author of 'The History of the Causes of the Civil War,' and of 'Human Nature,' than as a translator of the Iliad and the Odyssey. Dr. Gilbert Burnet, author of 'The History of his Own Times;' and Dr. Ralph Cudworth, author of 'The True Intellectual System of the Universe,' were likewise men of note. But one whose name is far more familiar than any writer of his time is John Bunyan, author of 'The Pilgrim's Progress.'

He was the son of a tinker, and was born

within a mile of Bedford town in the year
1628. He imbibed at an early age the spirit of
Puritanism, fought in the civil wars, took to
himself a wife, and turned preacher. Six
months after the merry monarch landed, Bunyan
was flung into Bedford gaol, where, rather
than refrain from puritanical discourses, in
the utterance of which he believed himself
divinely inspired, he remained, with some
short intervals of liberty, for twelve years.
When offered freedom at the price of silence,
he replied, 'If you let me out to-day, I will
preach to-morrow.' Nay, even in his confine-
ment he delivered sermons to his fellow-
prisoners; and presently he commenced to write.
His convictions leading him to attack the
liturgy of the Church of England, and the
religion of the Quakers, his productions became
popular amongst dissenters. At length, by an
act annulling the penal statutes against Protestant Nonconformists and Roman Catholics,
passed in 1671, he was liberated. When he left
prison he carried with him a portion of his
'Pilgrim's Progress,' which was soon after
completed and published, though at what date

remains uncertain. In 1678 a second edition was printed, and such was the growth of its popularity, that six editions were issued within the following four years.

Now he became famous, his lot was far different from what it had been; his sermons were heard by eager audiences, his counsel was sought by those in trouble, his prayers were regarded as the utterances of inspiration. Once a year he rode, attended by vast crowds, from Bedford Town to London City, that he might preach to those burdened by sin; and from the capital he made a circuit of the country, where he was hailed as a prophet. His life extended beyond the reign of King Charles; his influence lasted till his death.

CHAPTER XI.

Time's flight leaves the king unchanged.—The Rye House conspiracy. — Profligacy of the court. — The three duchesses.—The king is taken ill.—The capital in consternation.—Dr. Ken questions his majesty.—A Benedictine monk sent for.—Charles professes catholicity and receives the Sacraments.—Farewell to all.—His last night on earth.—Daybreak and death.—He rests in peace.

His majesty's habits changed but little with the flight of time. To the end of his reign the court continued brilliant and profligate. Wits, courtezans, and adventurers crowded the royal drawing-rooms, and conversed without restraint; the monarch pursued his pleasures with unsatiated zest, taking to himself two new mistresses, Lady Shannon and Catherine Peg, who respectively bore him a daughter and a son, duly created Countess of Yarmouth and Earl of Plymouth. For a while, indeed, a shadow fell upon the life of the merry monarch, when, in

1683, he was roused to a sense of danger by discovery of the Rye House conspiracy.

This foul plot, entered into by the Whigs on failure of the Exclusion Bill, had for its object the murder of his majesty and of the Duke of York. Before arriving at maturity its existence and intentions were revealed by one of the conspirators, when William Lord Russell, the Earl of Essex, and Algernon Sidney, second son of the Earl of Leicester, were arrested and charged with high treason. My Lord Essex died in the Tower by his own hand; Lord Russell was condemned on testimony of one witness, and duly executed; as was likewise Algernon Sidney, whose writings on Republicanism were used as evidence against him. On the revelation of this wicked scheme the country became wildly excited, and the king grievously afflicted. A melancholy seized upon his majesty, who stirred not abroad without double guards; and the private doors of Whitehall and avenues of the park were closed.

From this condition, however, he gradually recovered, and resumed his usual habits. Accordingly, we find him engaged in 'luxurious dalliance and prophaneness' with the Duchess of Mazarine, and visiting the Duchess of Portsmouth betimes in her chamber, where that bold and voluptuous woman, fresh risen from bed, sat in loose garments talking to the king and his gallants, the while her maids combed her beautiful hair.

'I can never forget,' says John Evelyn, writing on the 4th of February, 1685, 'the inexpressible luxury and prophaneness, gaming, and all dissoluteness, and as it were total forgetfullnesse of God (it being Sunday evening), which this day se'nnight I was witnesse of, the king sitting and toying with his concubines, Portsmouth, Cleveland, and Mazarine, etc., a French boy singing love songs in that glorious gallery, whilst about twenty of the greate courtiers and other dissolute persons were at basset round a large table, a bank of at least two thousand in gold before them, upon which two gentlemen who were with me made reflexions with astonishment. Six days after was all in the dust.'

For now the end of all things had come for Charles Stuart. It happened on the morning of the 2nd of February, 1685, the day being Monday, the king whilst in his bedroom was seized by an apoplectic fit, when crying out, he fell back in his chair, and lay as one dead. Wildly alarmed, his attendants summoned Dr. King, the physician in waiting, who immediately bled him, and had him carried to bed. Then tidings spread throughout the palace, that his majesty hovered betwixt life and death; which should claim him no man might say. Whereon the Duke of York hastened to his bedside, as did likewise the queen, her face blanched, her eyes wild with terror. His majesty after some time recovering consciousness, slowly realized his sad condition. Then he conceived a fear, the stronger as begotten by conviction, that the sands of his life had run their course. Throughout that day and the next he fainted frequently, and showed symptoms of epilepsy. On Wednesday he was cupped and bled in both jugulars; but on Thursday he was pronounced better, when the physicians, anxious to welcome hope, spoke of his probable recovery.

But, alas the same evening he grew restless, and signs of fever became apparent. Jesuits' powders, then of great repute, were given him, but with no good result. Complaining of a pain in his side, the doctors drew twelve ounces more of blood from him. Exhaustion then set in; all hope of life was over.

Meanwhile, the capital was in a state of dire consternation. Prayers for his majesty's recovery were offered up in all churches throughout the city; likewise in the royal chapels, where the clergy relieved each other every quarter of an hour. Crowds gathered by day and night without the palace gates, eager to learn the latest change in the king's condition from those who passed to and fro. Inside Whitehall all was confusion. Members of the Privy Council assembled in the room adjoining that where the monarch lay; politicians and ambassadors conversed in whispers in the disordered apartments; courtiers of all degrees flocked through the corridors bearing signs of deep concern upon their countenances.

And amongst others who sought his majesty's presence was the Archbishop of Canterbury, together with the Bishops of London, Durham, Ely, and Bath and Wells; all being anxious to render spiritual services to the king. Of these good men, Charles liked best Dr. Ken, Bishop of Bath and Wells, having most faith in his honesty. For, when his lordship was a prebend of Winchester, it had happened Charles passed through that city, accompanied by Nell Gwynne, when Dr. Ken refused to receive her beneath his roof even at the king's request. This proof of integrity so pleased his majesty, that he gave him the next vacant bishopric by way of reward. And now, his lordship being at hand, he read prayers for the Sick from out the Common Prayer Book for his benefit, until coming to that part where the dying are exhorted to make confession of their sins, when the bishop paused and said such was not obligatory. He then asked his majesty if he were sorry for the iniquities of his life? when the sick man, whose heart was exceeding heavy, replied he was; whereon the bishop pronounced absolution, and asked him if he would receive the Sacrament. To this Charles made no reply, until the same question had been repeated several times, when his majesty answered he would think of it.

The Duke of York, who stood by the while, noting the king's answer, and aware of his tendencies towards Catholicism, bade those who had gathered round stand aside; and then, bending over him, asked in a low tone if he might send for a priest. A look of unspeakable relief came into the king's face, and he answered, 'For God's sake do, brother, and lose no time.' Then another thought flashing across his mind, he said, 'But will not this expose you to much danger?' James made answer, 'Though it cost me my life I will bring you a priest.' He then hurried into the next room, where, among all the courtiers, he could find no man he could trust, save a foreigner, one Count Castelmachlor. Calling him aside, he secretly despatched him in search of a priest.

Between seven and eight o'clock that evening, Father Huddleston, the Benedictine friar who had aided the king's escape after the battle of Worcester, awaited at the queen's back stairs the signal to appear in his majesty's presence. The duke being made aware of the fact, announced it to the king, who thereon ordered all in his room to withdraw; but James, mindful that slander might afterwards charge him with killing his brother, begged the Earl of Bath, the lord of the bedchamber then in waiting, and the Earl of Feversham, captain of the guard, might stay—saying to the king it was not fitting he should be unattended in his weak condition. These gentlemen therefore remained. And no sooner had all others departed than the monk was admitted by a private entrance to the chamber. The king received him with great joy and satisfaction, stating he was anxious to die in the communion of the catholic church, and declaring he was sorry for the wrongs of his past life, which he yet hoped might be pardoned through the merits of Christ.

He then, as we read in the Stuart Papers, 'with exceeding compunction and tenderness of heart,' made an exact confession of his sins, after which he repeated an act of contrition, and received absolution. He next desired to have the other Sacraments of the church proper to his condition administered to him: on which the Benedictine asked if he desired to receive the Eucharist; eagerly he replied, 'If I am worthy pray fail not to let me have it.' Then Father Huddleston, after some exhortation, prepared to give him the Sacrament; when the dying man, struggling to raise himself, exclaimed, 'Let me meet my heavenly Lord in a better posture than lying in bed.' But the priest begged he would not move, and then gave him the Communion, which he received with every sign of fervour. And for some time he prayed earnestly, the monk and the duke kneeling by the while, silence obtaining in the room. This was presently broken by the sad and solemn tones of the priest's voice, reading a commendation of the soul to its Maker: the which being ended, the Benedictine, with tears in his eyes, took leave of his majesty. 'Ah,' said Charles, 'you once saved my body; you have now saved my soul.' Then the monk gave him his benediction, and departed as quietly as he had come.

Then those waiting without were once more admitted to the room, when Charles nerved himself to take a sad farewell of those around him. He first publicly thanked his brother for the services and affection he had ever rendered him through life, and extolled his obedience and submission to his commands. Giving him his keys, he said he had left him all he possessed, and prayed God would bless him with a happy and prosperous reign. Finally, he recommended all his children to him by name, excepting only the Duke of Monmouth, then in Holland, and suffering from the king's displeasure; and besought him to extend his kindness towards the Duchesses of Portsmouth and Cleveland; 'and do not,' said he, 'let poor Nelly starve.' Whilst these commands were addressed him, the duke had flung himself on his knees by the bedside, and, bursting into tears, kissed his brother's hand.

The queen, who had scarce left his majesty since the commencement of his illness, was at this time absent, her love and grief not permitting her to endure this afflicting scene. He spoke most tenderly of her; and when presently she sent a message praying he would pardon her absence in regard to her excessive grief, and forgive her withal if at any time she had offended him, he replied, 'Alas, poor woman! She beg my pardon?—I beg hers, with all my heart.' He next summoned his children to him, one by one, and addressing them with words of advice, embraced them heartily, and blessed them fervently.

And he being the Lord's anointed, the bishops present besought he would give them his benediction likewise, and all that were present, and in them the whole body of his subjects; in compliance with which request he, with some difficulty, raised himself, and all falling on their knees, he blessed them fervently. Then they arose and departed.

Silence fell upon the palace; the night wore slowly by. Charles tossed upon his bed racked with pain, but no complaint escaped his lips. Those who watched him in the semi-darkened room heard him ask God to accept his sufferings in atonement for his sins. Then, speaking aloud, he declared himself weary of life, and hoped soon to reach a better world. Courteous to the last, he begged pardon for the trouble he gave, inasmuch as he was long in dying. And anon he slumbered, and quickly woke again in agony, and prayed with zeal. Never had time moved with slower passage for him; not hours, but weeks, seemed to elapse between each stroke of the clock; and yet around him was darkness and tardy night. But after much weary waiting, morning was at hand, the timepiece struck six. 'Draw the curtains' said the dying man, 'that I may once more see day.' The grey light of a February dawn, scarce brightened to eastward a cheerless sky; but he hailed this herald of sunrise with infinite relief and terrible regret; relief, that he had lived to see another day; regret, that no more morns should break for him.

His soul tore itself from his body with fierce struggles and bitter pain. It was hard for him to die, but he composed himself to enter eternity 'with the piety becoming a christian, and the resolution becoming a king,' as his brother narrates. About ten o'clock on Friday morning, February 6th, 1685, he found relief in unconsciousness; before midday chimed he was dead. He had reached the fifty-fifth year of his life, and the twenty-fifth year of his reign.

His illegitimate progeny was numerous, numbering fifteen, besides those who died in infancy. These were the Duke of Monmouth, and a daughter married to William Sarsfield, children of Lucy Walters; the Dukes of Southampton, Grafton, and Northumberland, the Countesses of Litchfield and of Sussex, and a daughter Barbara who became a nun, children of the Duchess of Cleveland; the Duke of Richmond, son of the Duchess of Portsmouth; the Duke of St. Albans, and a son James, children of Nell Gwynn; Lady Derwentwater, daughter of Moll Davis; the Countess of Yarmouth, daughter of Lady Shannon; and the Earl of Plymouth, son of Catherine Peg.

For seven days the remains of the late king lay in state; on the eighth they were placed in the tomb. This was of necessity accomplished in a semi-private manner; for by reason of his majesty dying in the catholic religion, his brother considered it desirable the ceremonies prescribed for the occasion by the English church should be dispensed with. Therefore, in order to avoid disputes or scandal, the king was laid in the tomb without ostentation. At night his remains were carried from the painted chamber in Westminster sanctuary to the abbey. The procession was headed by the servants of the nobility, of James II., and his queen, of the dowager queen, and of the late king; followed by the barons, bishops, and peers according to their rank; the officers of the household, and the

Archbishop of Canterbury. Then came all that was mortal of his late majesty, borne under a canopy of velvet, supported by six gentlemen of the privy chamber, the pall being held by six earls. Prince George of Denmark—subsequently husband of Queen Anne—acted as chief mourner, attended by the Dukes of Somerset and Beaufort, and sixteen earls. One of the kings of Arms carried the crown and cushion, the train being closed by the king's band of gentlemen pensioners, and the yeomen of the guard.

At the entrance to the church, the dean and prebendaries, attended by torch bearers, and followed by a surpliced choir, met the remains, and joined the procession, the slow pacing figures of which seemed spectral in this hour and place; then the sad cortege passed solemnly through the grey old abbey, the choir chanting sorrowfully the while, the yellow flare of torches marking the prevailing gloom. And being come to the chapel of Henry VII., the body of the merry monarch was suffered there to rest in peace.

THE END.

WORKS BY THE SAME AUTHOR.

'Mr. Fitzgerald Molloy has a gift and a charm which are peculiarly his own. He is a Voyan, a clairvoyant even, from a literary point of view. He sees things—not in the present but in the past—so clearly, grasps them so tenaciously, and reproduces them so vividly that they come to us without any of the dust and rust of time.'—G. A. S. in 'Echoes of the Week.'

'Mr. Molloy's style is bright and fluent, picturesque and animated, and he tells his stories with unquestionable skill and vivacity.'—ATHENÆUM.

COURT LIFE BELOW STAIRS;
OR, LONDON UNDER THE FIRST GEORGES.
By J. FITZGERALD MOLLOY.
One Vol., Crown 8vo. Price 6s.

'No truer or more vivid picture of the last century has been written. The value of the present work as a picture of Court manners under the first Georges is greatly enhanced by the fact that, as far as possible, it is historically correct.'—*Morning Post.*

'Mr. Molloy's pages contain abundance of amusing anecdote. He writes in a brisk and fluent style.'—*Athenæum.*

'Mr. Molloy produces some curious anecdotes which have not before appeared in print, and he is always lively.'—*Pall Mall Gazette.*

'Concerning the amusing incidents and royal quarrels, the domestic scenes, the brilliant and immoral courtiers he has much to say, and, moreover, says it in a witty and pleasant manner. The anecdotes of Pope and Addison, Swift and Steele, Colley Cibber, Gay, Congreve, Susanna Centlivre, Lady Mary Wortley Montagu, and others are all interesting.'—*Sunday Times.*

'Though Mr. Molloy has not been alone in recognising the value of the Wentworth correspondence, it has been for the first time brought by him before the notice of the general public, and his quotations cannot fail to awaken genuine interest. . . . . In these sketches of Court Life there is no lack of rollicking vivacity to carry the reader along interested in the narrative.'—*Academy.*

'Mr. Molloy has evidently found a subject congenial to his taste and fitting to his lively and facile pen.'—*Daily News.*

'Well written, full of anecdote, and with its facts admirably grouped, this excellent work will prove of the greatest value to all who desire to know what manner of men the first Electors of Hanover who came here really were. . . . . Contemporary history of the time treated of is so interwoven that the record is one complete and happily-framed narrative. . . . . In fine, Mr. Molloy's work as a history seems all that it should be.'—*Daily Telegraph.*

WARD & DOWNEY, PUBLISHERS,
12, YORK STREET, COVENT GARDEN, LONDON.

COURT LIFE BELOW STAIRS;

OR, LONDON UNDER THE LAST GEORGES.

By J. Fitzgerald Molloy.

One Vol., Crown 8vo. Price 6s.

'These volumes are quite equal to the earlier ones. Mr. Molloy's style is crisp, and carries the reader along; his portraits of the famous men and women of the time are etched with care, and his narrative rises to intensity and dramatic impressiveness as he follows the latter days of Queen Caroline.'—*British Quarterly Review.*

'The narrative is fluent and amusing, and is far more instructive than nine-tenths of the novels published nowadays.'—*St. James's Gazette.*

' Mr. Molloy's narrative is concise, and exhibits a wide acquaintance with the men and manners of the age. The anecdotes of famous men of fashion, wits, fools, or knaves introduced are amusing, and several not generally known enliven the pages.'—*Morning Post.*

'Full of facts bearing on every subject under consideration, and abounding with anecdotes of gay and witty debauchees.'—*Daily Telegraph.*

' Clever, graphic, and reliable pictures of the Court and social life under the last Georges.'—*Sunday Times.*

' What Pepys has done for the Stuarts Mr. Molloy has done for their Hanoverian successors. The result of his arduous investigations is one of the most interesting works which has ever come under our notice. It is impossible to open the books at any part without feeling an overpowering desire to continue the perusal.'—*Newcastle Chronicle.*

' With consummate skill Mr. Molloy carries his readers through the seventy eventful years comprised within his story; and not until the last chapter is reached will the reader lay aside this work. The volumes will doubtless be in as great demand at the libraries as were the earlier ones, with which the Prince of Wales declared he had been greatly amused.'—*Dorset County Chronicle.*

WARD & DOWNEY, Publishers,
12, YORK STREET, COVENT GARDEN, LONDON.

In Picture Boards. Price 2s.

IT IS NO WONDER.

By J. Fitzgerald Molloy.

'An exceedingly powerful and fascinating story.'—*Daily Telegraph.*

'The heroine is depicted with considerable dramatic force. The story contains some pleasant sketches of Bohemian life in London, and is cleverly told.'—*Scotsman.*

'There is a freshness and liveliness about the story. It is smartly written and skilfully managed; but Mr. Molloy is not content with so much success. He must needs introduce a great passion and enforce what doubtless he thinks a great moral.'—*Pall Mall Gazette.*

'The story is very well told, and we meet in the course of it with sketches of life which strike the mind by their incisiveness and originality. . . . In the delineation of such characters as those of Felice Stanning and Marcus Phillips the painter the author shows himself capable of excellent work. But perhaps the best and most kindly study in the novel is that of the vulgar, warm-hearted American, Mrs. W. Achilles Lordson; this is natural, and shows considerable sense of humour.'—*Morning Post.*

'The driest and boniest of reviewers will not be able to deny that Mr. Molloy can write in a pleasant style, and describe contemporary society in a manner which, if a little free, is undoubtedly easy. His book displays considerable power of distinct character-drawing. The earlier part of the heroine's story is told playfully and sympathetically, and the scenes of her Bohemian life are charming. . . . Mr. Molloy describes the scampish captain, her father, with minuteness and humour.'—*Daily News.*

'Mr. Molloy has maintained in this work the reputation which his "Merely Players" and some others of his writings have obtained for him. It is not only that the story is one of sustained interest, but it has furnished him with a wide field for the exercise of a power in which he excels—the portraiture of distinctive character. . . . It is so replete with interesting and descriptive passages and with thoughtful reflections that it cannot fail to be read with interest.'—*Bristol Mercury.*

WARD & DOWNEY, Publishers,
12, YORK STREET, COVENT GARDEN, LONDON.

www.ingramcontent.com/pod-product-compliance
Lightning Source LLC
Chambersburg PA
CBHW021208230426
43667CB00006B/607